THE COMPLETE
DuPage County
Trail Guide

A PRAIRIE COMPASS GUIDE

THE COMPLETE
DuPage County Trail Guide

Your Total Reference to DuPage County Forest Preserve Trails and DuPage Community Trails

BY

BILL WEIDNER

Prairie Compass Publishing

OTTAWA, ILLINOIS

Contents

Regional Trails

City and Village Bikeways, Pathways, and Trails

Menacing and Not-So-Menacing Road Cycling Routes

Acknowledgments

Writing a book is like hiking, biking or skiing along a long trail. It is a solitary experience for the most part but in order to be successful and get the most out of the experience one shares the experience and relies on a whole lot of people. One listens to them, uses their ideas and applies their suggestions. Many of my friends and colleagues have acted as my guides every step of the way.

I have also drawn specific information from several agencies' and institutions' informational materials. I am indebted to all of them.

I greatly appreciate everyone's kind input. Thank you all for your knowledge and expertise. If you are not mentioned and think you should be, I beg your pardon. You are probably right.

With thanks and love to my family: Alice, who walked, hiked, biked and cross-country skied many trails with me, reviewed material and offered many suggestions for the book's improvement and countless forms of kindness and love, and Amie, Marian and Katie who traveled many trail routes in sleds, Snuglis© and bike seats until they could transport themselves. Their support and encouragement always inspire me to do good work.

The creation and development of this book took a lot of bicycle riding and great comrades rode on down the trails with me. I am grateful for jogging pal and trail talker Mike Duquette and the biking friend boys: Dave Brummel and Matt Wiesbrock.; the trail hounds: Kirby, Cochise and Spooky; and my Arabian saddle mates: Satin, Sundance and Shala.

Many colleagues provided helpful support and well-researched information, graphic technical assistance and documentation about the DuPage County development plans, natural and cultural resources, bike routes, trail systems and forest preserves. Thank you to Jayne Bohner, Audra Bonnet, Deanna Eichenauer, Elmhurst Bike Club, Deborah Fagan, Terry Fortman, Dan Gooch, Tim Houston, Ross Hill, Kevin Horsfall, Andrea Hoyt, Scott Kobal, Don LaBrose, Wayne Lampa, Kevin Luby, Brent Manning, Jack MacRae, Kathy McManus, Scott Meister, Naperville Bike Club, Mike Palazzetti, Rachel Reklau, Beth Schirott and Todd Volker.

Maurice Weiser and Dick Todd generously allowed me to publish their original photographs. I am overwhelmed by their generosity.

Introduction

Trails are alive! Pathways are constantly changing and growing under our feet, bike tires and skis.

When you think that you have covered all routes and described them in detail, a plant grows, fog slips in or you hit a cool spot. Agencies and communities change routes, add signs, design and construct bridges, prune intersections, plant trees and shrubs, improve turning radii on hairpin turns, and widen or meander new trails. Our pathways always change. It is their nature.

For thousands of years, people followed trails of buffalo, deer and other game, veered off them and took short cuts to arrive sooner rather than later. Early 1800s settlers in prairie schooners crossed rivers and streams where a gravel vein on a creek or river bottom exposed a solid, rocky and shallow crossing. Locating convenient and safe crossings saved time and provided a much less precarious route. Marshes and fens were skirted and passage across firm prairie and savanna sod allowed stagecoaches to cover seventy-five miles in a 24-hour day of travel. Even half the distance would be considered "pretty fair going," according to Joy Morton's written introduction to *Chicago's Highways Old and New* by Milo M. Quaife.

Today, trails are different, although they can still offer challenges and adventures galore. It is my intention to offer places to get away from life's everyday stressors, or like the Club Med advertisement stated offer "an antidote to civilization." Descriptions of paths to follow that will refresh your soul and spirit. We all deserve these fantastic and invigorating trail experiences. Recent studies indicate that more contact with nature is beneficial for our health and psyche.

Hopefully this compilation of more than 250 miles of trail descriptions and listings of resources will provide you with the right amount of information you will need to explore the many routes through DuPage County. Be sure you take time and enjoy the route!

DuPage Forest Preserve District Map

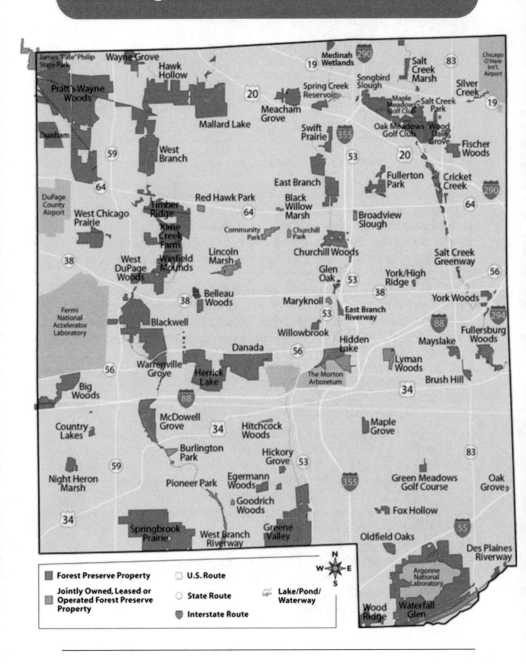

Forest Preserve and State Park Trails

Roy C. Blackwell Forest Preserve Trail

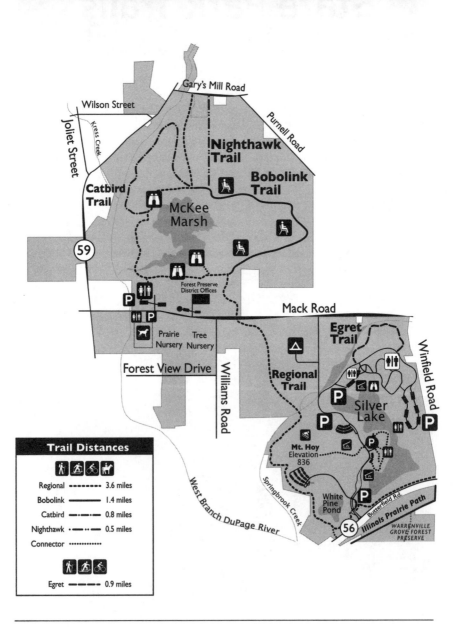

Gary's Mill Road

Wilson Street

Purnell Road

Joliet Street

Kress Creek

Nighthawk Trail

Bobolink Trail

Catbird Trail

McKee Marsh

59

Forest Preserve District Offices

Mack Road

Prairie Nursery   Tree Nursery

Egret Trail

Forest View Drive

Williams Road

Regional Trail

Silver Lake

Winfield Road

Mt. Hoy Elevation 836

West Branch DuPage River

Springbrook Creek

White Pine Pond

Butterfield Rd.

Illinois Prairie Path

56

WARRENVILLE GROVE FOREST PRESERVE

Trail Distances

Regional	-------- 3.6 miles
Bobolink	———— 1.4 miles
Catbird	—·—·— 0.8 miles
Nighthawk	·—··— 0.5 miles
Connector	·············

Egret	—·—·— 0.9 miles

2

Roy C. Blackwell Forest Preserve Trail

WARRENVILLE

TRAIL LENGTH

The length of the trail at Blackwell is 6.3 miles.

TRAIL SURFACE

Crushed limestone.

The Blackwell trail is groomed for diagonal and skate cross-country skiing when there is adequate snow cover.

LOCATION

The Roy C. Blackwell Forest Preserve is in Warrenville. The main entrance is on the north side of Butterfield Road (Illinois Route 56), one-quarter mile west of Winfield Road and one mile east of Illinois Route 59. Five large parking lots are located within this main area of the forest preserve. There is an additional parking area near McKee Marsh located on the north side of Mack road, between Illinois Route 59 and Williams Road.

TRAILHEAD LOCATIONS

There is no shortage of parking at Blackwell Forest Preserve. Bicyclists, hikers, cross-country skiers, fishing enthusiasts, picnickers and campers can park anywhere in the main parking areas on the north side of Butterfield Road (Illinois Route 56). The parking lots are near the picnic areas, shelters, campground, flush toilets, vending machines and boat rental building.

There is also a parking lot near McKee Marsh on the north side of Mack Road, which offers access to the natural areas and primitive restrooms. Both locations offer easy access to the regional trail.

TRAIL DESCRIPTION

The Blackwell trail system has a variety of opportunities for lovers of the outdoors. The trails include a 3.6-mile section of the regional trail that connects to the Illinois Prairie Path, trails at Herrick Lake Forest Preserve, Warrenville Grove Forest Preserve and the West DuPage River Trail that extends south to McDowell Grove Forest Preserve in Naperville and points beyond. The rapidly developing West DuPage River Corridor Trail will eventually extend north and south along the West Branch of the DuPage River for approximately twenty-four miles.

The Blackwell Forest Preserve trail includes both long and short-distanced hill climbs. The trail offers terrific hiking and bicycling opportunities. A biker or on skier can cruise and glide on the back sides of hills as the trail curls and weaves throughout a diverse landscape of oak woods, lakes, wetlands and open grasslands. By studying a Blackwell brochure or Illinois Prairie Path map you can design a ride, ski or hike that will provide an hour-long jaunt or a route to the Illinois Prairie Path for an all-day endurance ride. In fact if you want to make a weekend out of it, Blackwell has a fantastic family campground with showers and electricity. There is also a youth group campground without all the modern trappings.

If you want to have a real serious aerobic activity and enjoy a fitness extravaganza run or walk up and down Mount Hoy a few times. Mount Hoy is a former landfill that rises about 150 feet off the pancake flat terrain. It will certainly get your ticker going and you'll probably feel some stiffness in your leg muscles the next day!

Blackwell's McKee Marsh area includes interpretive trail signs, two observation decks and a bird blind that entice trekkers to learn about the rich natural history and ecological significance of the woods, waters and wildlife.

TRAVELER'S NOTEBOOK

There are ample picnic sites with or without shelters located around the shoreline of Silver Lake.

Need a snack? There are vending machines at the boat rental area, which is open on weekends in the spring and fall and daily during the summer season.

Need a break from your bike? You can rent a rowboat with or without an electric trolling motor or a canoe during the summer season.

Bike or hike to Silver Lake, a sixty-acre fishing hotspot. Loaner fishing poles can be requested and are available for free on a "first-come, first-served" basis. Fishermen who are 16 years of age or older should be sure to have a fishing license. Worms can be purchased at the concession vending area. Try you luck and cast your line from a pier or rent a boat. Canoes, kayaks and rowboats are available daily during the summer and on weekends during the spring and fall. Catching a trophy bass or fat catfish from a kayak can be a blast.

During summer, bikers and hikers can have a picnic at one of the lakeside tables or shelters. Or choose to spend the entire weekend in one of the sixty family campsites available at the campground. Campsites include a parking pad, fire ring and picnic table. There are campsites suitable for tents, trailers and motor homes. Restrooms with showers and campsites with electricity are also available. Beer, wine and all other alcohol-laced libations are forbidden. For permit and current fee information, call (630) 933-7248.

TRAIL TALK

On a hot muggy summer day in 1977, Gary Jones, an employee with the forest preserve, operated a heavy piece of machinery called a drag line and dug scoops of blue clay from under the black soil to use as a sealant for Blackwell's swim beach. Three kids watched. And as they watched they observed what looked like a long wooden stump stick out from the bucket of earthen clay. After taking a closer look, the appearance of unusual bones came into view. News spread quickly that bones from a 13,300 year-old woolly mammoth had been discovered. Everybody in the area knew them as "Jones Bones" and scientific institutions in the region offered helpful advice as more than 1,000 bone fragments were removed for study by a Northern Illinois University research group. Unfortunately the skull, teeth and front limbs were not recovered and either washed away or sank and decomposed in the mud.

Nobody knows how the Blackwell Mammoth perished. Experts have suggested that the animal may have become mired in the wet, mucky soil and could not pull itself free. It is unlikely that the beast was a victim of early hunters although in Kenosha County, Wisconsin, scientists have located mammoth-butchering sites.

Today, after the creation of McKee Marsh, the precise location where "Jones Bones" were found is now under water. The bones have been assembled as much as possible, to form a skeleton and are on display at Fullersburg Woods Nature Center in Oak Brook. It is an interesting exhibit and offers additional details about prehistoric mega-fauna that once roamed DuPage County.

FOR MORE INFORMATION

Visit the Forest Preserve District of DuPage County website at www.dupageforest.com or telephone (630) 933-7200.

Churchill Woods Forest Preserve Trail

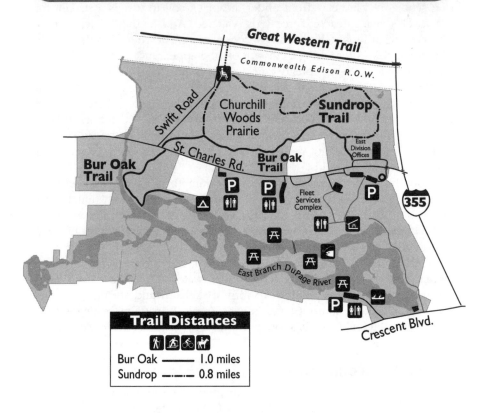

Great Western Trail

Commonwealth Edison R.O.W.

Churchill Woods Prairie

Sundrop Trail

Swift Road

St. Charles Rd.

Bur Oak Trail

Bur Oak Trail

East Division Offices

Fleet Services Complex

East Branch DuPage River

355

Crescent Blvd.

Trail Distances

Bur Oak ——— 1.0 miles
Sundrop –·–·– 0.8 miles

Churchill Woods Forest Preserve Trail

2

GLEN ELLYN

TRAIL LENGTH

2.66 miles

TRAIL SURFACE

Combination of mostly mowed turf and some crushed limestone.

DIRECTIONS

Located in Glen Ellyn there are two parking areas on the south side of St. Charles Road with easy access to the trail. The lots are located approximately one-quarter of a mile and one-half mile west of Illinois Route 53. There is another small four or five car lot along the east side of Swift Road a couple hundred yards north of St. Charles Road.

TRAILHEAD LOCATIONS

The Churchill Woods Forest Preserve trails in Glen Ellyn are on the north side and south side of St. Charles Road between Swift Road and Interstate 355. Hikers and bikers may park in the lot that is approximately one-quarter mile west of Illinois Route 53 on the south side of St. Charles Road.

Trekkers can take the underpass to the Sundrop and Burr Oak trails that loop around the prairie. Another trail access point is the small gravel lot on the east side of Swift Road north of St. Charles Road next to a Commonwealth Edison facility. This small parking area is close to the Great Western Trail that crosses Swift Road a hundred yards north of the lot.

TRAIL DESCRIPTION

This forest preserve offers a shorter trail. The area has a high quality woodlot comprised of burr oaks, black maples, walnuts and a few scattered white oaks and exhibits a large-scale fully restored prairie. A late summer ride at this preserve will be satisfying, although covering the distance on a road bike is not recommended. There are several state endangered plants and many monarch, viceroy and red spotted purple butterflies floating and winging around at the prairie. Bird and wildlife watching is also very good. During the spring and summer mornings watch for deep blue indigo bunting near the woodlot and prairie edge.

The trail across Churchill Woods Prairie and through the woods is mostly flat with a few mild undulations over its route to the East Branch of

7

the DuPage River. There is one long steady medium steep hill that rises uphill from the river to the northwest section of the preserve. Once at the top it offers a sweeping view of the prairie and oak woodlands as you look toward the DuPage River valley.

This trail can be traveled on a mountain bike in an hour or less and makes for a great location for a relaxing recess ride or lunch break tour away from office stressors. The mostly turf trail crosses under St. Charles Road through a tunnel on the route's east section and crosses over St. Charles Road on the trail route's west section. Skirting the edge of the East Branch of the DuPage River for approximately one-half mile, it offers pleasant placid scenes of families and couples relaxing in the picnic areas and fishing from the riverbank. Great blue herons, mallards and wood ducks call this area home.

TRAVELER'S NOTEBOOK

The looped trail system showcases this sixty-acre, specially designated, Illinois Nature Preserve. It is the one and only DuPage County Forest Preserve to receive Illinois Nature Preserve status. This designation of the Illinois Natural Areas Preservation Act provides additional legal protection to plants and animals living together in rare natural communities. According to the conservation statutes the natural lands and waters are ". . . known as habitats for rare and vanishing species; as places of historic and natural interest and scenic beauty as living museums of the native landscapes wherein one may envision and experience primeval conditions in a wilderness-like environment. They also contribute generally to the public health and welfare and the environmental quality of the vitality of the state. . . ."

The prairie was the first natural area in DuPage County to be designated an Illinois Nature Preserve. It was originally a wet mesic prairie with saturated soils and moisture-loving plants like the blue flag iris. It is assumed that the construction of Interstate 355 and other diversions on private land to the east has led toward much drier conditions on the prairie. The construction has forever changed the moisture conditions on the prairie's landscape. It remains to be seen how the plant and animal life will change and adapt as time marches on.

Seasonal flooding in this prairie is not likely any more. There has been a reduction of the moisture loving plants and some plant species have completely disappeared from the prairie community. Reed canary grass, an unwanted invasive species has rapidly advanced into sections of the prairie. Land managers wage constant botanical battle trying to fight back the advance of this plant and the aggressive buckthorn tree. The salt and sediment washing off the roadsides bordering the prairie has also negatively impacted the native plant species. The most significant of the losses has been the complete disappearance of the federally endangered eastern prairie fringed orchid. This loss of a plant species has occurred despite prescribed burning, herbicide treatments and the good work of natural resource volunteers.

TRAIL TALK

Many historical references refer to a sizable village of as many as 500 Potawatomi Indians that were encamped along the banks of the East Branch of DuPage River during the early 1800s at the present day site of Churchill Woods Forest Preserve. Here the Indians were protected from the sun's summer glare, and the shade provided a cooling effect. During winter the wind was blocked and people were protected from extreme cold and raging snowstorms. Food and medicinal plants were located and harvested in these same woodlands. These woodlands were also revered for their beauty-places so well respected that they buried their relatives under the canopy of trees. The Potawatomi land holdings in the Great Lakes region were sold and by 1835 most of the natives had been dispersed from the area.

As more people came to DuPage County, more demands were placed on the woodland resource. Changes to the woodland's importance took place. Between 1821 and 1840, the U.S. Government Land Office Public Land Survey was conducted in DuPage County. During that period, eighty percent of the county was prairie with the remainder being wooded in areas called barrens, scattered timber and timber. Oak trees once revered for their shelter and habitat were cut down for their resources.

In the middle of the nineteenth century many ancient oak trees in this area were felled and then sawed into planks for use in the construction of plank roads and fees were charged to travel upon plank roads. Early pioneer Winslow Churchill is said to have complained about the traffic noise from horse-drawn vehicles that clattered over the plank covered St. Charles Road. It kept him awake at night. You can still easily hear traffic noise coming from the Interstate 355 toll road when you are out and about in Churchill Woods Forest Preserve. Some things never change.

FOR MORE INFORMATION

Visit the Forest Preserve District of DuPage County website at www.dupageforest.com or telephone (630) 933-7200.

Cricket Creek Forest Preserve Trail

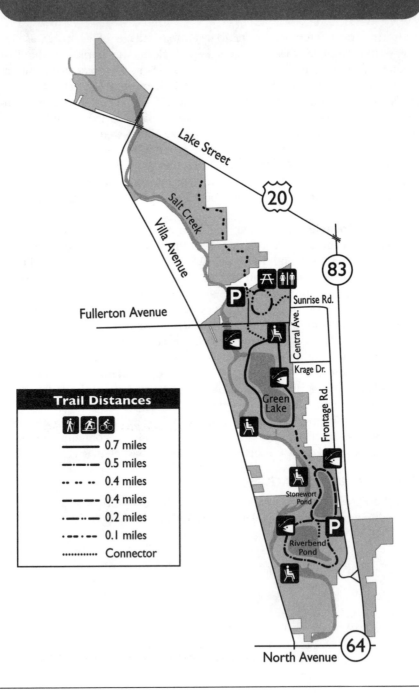

Trail Distances

🚶 🎿 🚴	
———————	0.7 miles
—·—·—·	0.5 miles
·· ·· ··	0.4 miles
— — — —	0.4 miles
·—·—··—	0.2 miles
·—·· ·—··	0.1 miles
·············	Connector

Lake Street

Salt Creek

Villa Avenue

20

83

Fullerton Avenue

Sunrise Rd.

Central Ave.

Krage Dr.

Green Lake

Frontage Rd.

Stonewort Pond

Riverbend Pond

North Avenue

64

Cricket Creek Forest Preserve Trail

3

ADDISON

TRAIL LENGTH

Short looped trails totaling 1.9 miles encircle three flood retention areas at Cricket Creek.

TRAIL SURFACE

Crushed limestone.

LOCATION

Cricket Creek Forest Preserve is in Addison west of Illinois Route 83, east of Villa Avenue, south of Lake Street (Illinois Route 20) and north of North Avenue (Illinois Route 64).

TRAILHEAD LOCATIONS

The main entrance is located on the north side of Fullerton Avenue one block east of Villa Avenue and south of Lake Street (U.S. Route 20). A second smaller parking lot is located on the west side of the Frontage Road one-quarter mile south of Fullerton Avenue.

TRAIL DESCRIPTION

The trail is as level as a bowling alley and it circles around each of three floodwater retention lakes found within the preserve. The trail is raised up on the top of a berm and out in the open with little shade. It can be windy out there. It is near Illinois Route 83 and traffic noise is 24 hours a day, seven days a week, 365 days a year.

There is also a short paved looped trail that encircles the picnic area and reservable shelter making it easy to negotiate for beginner bicyclists, wheelchairs and strollers. Benches are located at different spots along the trail so visitors can relax and view this forest preserve's pleasant scenery.

TRAVELER'S NOTEBOOK

Massive development within the Salt Creek flood plain has caused considerable flooding and property damage in the creek's valley. After years of flooding an entire subdivision of seventy-five houses was purchased in 1970. The houses were demolished in order to restore a part of Salt Creek's floodplain. Many of the homes had watermarks half way up on their bay windows!

Cricket Creek is considered to be DuPage County's first wetland mitigation bank and includes three shallow lakes named Green Lake, Stonewort Pond and Riverbend Pond. The lakes depth is approximately ten feet deep but during flood events the depth and size of these lakes swells and shrinks as Salt Creek's floodwater rise and fall. Fish species include; largemouth bass, bluegill, channel catfish, crappie, green sunfish, carp, black bullhead and flathead catfish.

TRAIL TALK

The Forest Preserve District and the Illinois Department of Transportation purchase were not without controversy. One holdout homeowner did not vacate until the demolition crew, which included a bulldozer, surrounded his residence! The flood control facility has proven to be a success by transforming the frequently flooded housing development into a beautiful 183-acre forest preserve on the east side of DuPage County where because of rapid development there is a shortage of natural open space areas.

FOR MORE INFORMATION

Visit the Forest Preserve District of DuPage County website at www.dupageforest.com or telephone (630) 933-7200.

THINGS YOU SHOULD KNOW ABOUT DUPAGE COUNTY

- Nearly 12,000 years ago the Wisconsin Glacier slid out of DuPage County leaving it flat and with an average elevation of 750 feet above sea level.

- The bones of an 11,000 year-old mastodon were unearthed near Churchill Woods Forest Preserve in Glen Ellyn and in 1977 a woolly mammoth that was approximately 13,000 years old was dug up at Blackwell Forest Preserve in Warrenville. In 2005, mastodon teeth, ivory and bone fragments were discovered at a restoration site in Pratt's Wayne Forest Preserve.

- French explorers Louis Joliet and Father Jacques Marquette were the first European explorers and crossed into southeastern DuPage County near the Des Plaines River in 1673.

- Butterfield Road (Illinois Route 56) and Warrenville Roads were once Blackfoot and Potawatomi Indian trails.

- In the 1830s it took more than three days to get from DuPage County to Chicago. During rainy weather the muddy tall grass prairies and streams would be difficult to pass across.

- McDowell Grove was a radar training station during World War II.

- Waterfall Glen has a beautiful waterfall but the most biologically diverse forest preserve is named after Seymour "Bud" Waterfall an early president of the forest preserve district's board.

- There is an artesian well at Waterfall Glen.

- Skunk cabbage is the earliest plant to bloom. It generates enough heat to burst through snow cover in early February.

- Blues great Muddy Water lived in Westmont.

- John and Jim Belushi lived in Wheaton during their youth.

- The first recorded traffic death in DuPage County took place on October 17, 1912 when the driver of a 1911 White was killed when his automobile overturned while allowing a mule wagon to pass on a muddy road.

- On June 7, 1915 DuPage County became the second county in the state to establish a forest preserve district and the fifth county park system in the country.

- In 1899, the Chicago, Aurora & Elgin, an electric interurban railroad, began operations moving commuters from the suburbs to Chicago and back.

- The Chicago, Aurora & Elgin ceased operations on July 3, 1957 and years later the railroad bed would become the base for the Illinois Prairie Path.

- Glen Ellyn is a town that has had many names. Babcock's Grove, DuPage Center, Stacy's Corners, Newton's Station, Danby and Prospect Park were predecessors to the village's present official name of Glen Ellyn.

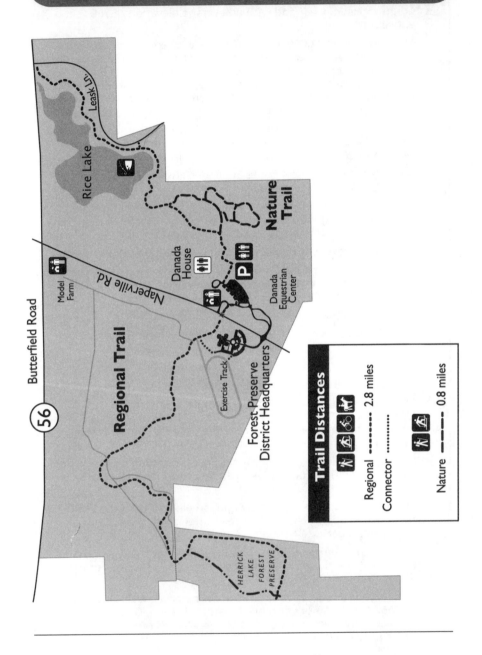

Trail Distances

Regional ------- 2.8 miles

Connector ·········

Nature — — — 0.8 miles

Rice Lake

Leask Ln.

Nature Trail

Danada House

Danada Equestrian Center

Model Farm

Naperville Rd.

Butterfield Road

56

Regional Trail

Exercise Track

Forest Preserve District Headquarters

HERRICK LAKE FOREST PRESERVE

Danada
Forest Preserve Trail

4

W H E A T O N

TRAIL LENGTH

2.8 miles with linkage to several miles of additional forest preserve trails and the Illinois Prairie Path.

TRAIL SURFACE

Crushed limestone.

The Danada trail is groomed for diagonal and skate cross-country skiing when there is adequate snow cover.

LOCATION

Danada Forest Preserve is in Wheaton and the parking lots are located on east and west side of Naperville Road, approximately 0.9 mile south of Butterfield Road (Illinois Route 56) and 0.75 mile north of Interstate 88.

TRAILHEAD LOCATIONS

Access points to the trail are located on the east and west sides of Naperville Road. To the east are the parking lots for the Danada Equestrian Center, 3 S. 503 Naperville Road and Danada House, 3 S. 501 Naperville Road. On the west side of Naperville Road, directly across the street from the eastern entrance is the parking lot at the Forest Preserve District of DuPage County's Administrative offices at 3 S. 580 Naperville Road in Wheaton.

TRAIL DESCRIPTION

The trail is about 2.8 miles in length and connects with the Herrick Lake Forest Preserve trail system and extends onward to the west, dead-ending conveniently near an Oberweis Ice Cream shop and Danada East Mall to the east. At Danada Forest Preserve shopping, eating and wilderness travel offers the best of all worlds to the trail traveler. Eventually a trail connection through the Morton Arboretum will add to the easterly route but as it stands now having the trail end at a great ice cream store is a nice oasis to arrive at after pedaling a long distance on a hot afternoon.

The trail through the 753-acre Danada Forest Preserve is a beautiful and fun ride. It runs west from Leask Lane and serpentines up and down hill past thirty-six acre Rice Lake and into the restored woodland named

15

Parson's Grove. Many spring native wildflowers bloom in this area, including bloodroot, wild geranium and trout lily. The woodlot is a near perfect depiction of what the groves in this area would have looked like two hundred years ago when the settlers first arrived. If you want to take a close look at this rare oak savanna area, there is a nature trail (for hiking only) that is approximately one mile. Bicyclists will need to dismount since this trail is narrow and exclusively for hikers, bird watchers and for those who want to take a close look at nature's beauty and diversity.

As you glide west through the woods you may hear the whinny and nickers of horses. Bicyclists should use caution and be under control at all times. Be sure to be courteous and announce your presence from a distance so that horse and riders will not be startled.

This forest preserve was once a private estate owned by Daniel and Ada Rice, the Kentucky-style barn of this former estate is now home to the Danada Equestrian Center. You will undoubtedly see horses out in the white fenced pastures and the Danada House will come into view as you ride west and continue through the Naperville Road underpass. Before connecting to the Herrick Lake trails you will pass the half-mile oval thoroughbred exercise track complete with its starting gates, a 35-acre restored prairie and a wetland complex. The woods, prairie and marshes attract a wide variety of wildlife. Keep your eyes open for coyote, great blue herons, bobolinks, red-tailed hawks, and white-tailed deer and of course, horses.

TRAVELER'S NOTEBOOK

Danada is the former home of Daniel and Ada L. Rice. Daniel Rice made his fortune on the grain commodities market and purchased the property in 1929. In 1939, construction began on the nineteen-room mansion, greenhouse, storage sheds, swimming pool, skeet and trap range, employee boarding homes and formal gardens of peonies and roses. The estate was originally a 1,350-acre working farm and was blanketed with an apple orchard, crops of wheat, corn and livestock. It was the thoroughbred racehorses, though that won the hearts and was the pride of the Rice family.

In the mid-1940s, the Rices constructed the 26-stall Kentucky-style barn and a half-mile oval racetrack used for exercising and training their racehorses. In 1949, the Rices entered their first horse in the Kentucky Derby. But it wasn't until 1965 that another of their horses, Lucky Debonair crossed the finish line in Louisville with the third-fastest time in the history of the race. It was jockey Willie Shoemaker's third Kentucky Derby victory that set him apart from other jockeys of the time. In 1966, another Danada Farm horse, named Abdicator placed second at the Kentucky Derby.

The Forest Preserve District of DuPage County purchased about half the Rice property in 1980. Prior to the purchase there was a very active and successful group of neighbors and DuPage County residents who formed the "Save the Rice Farm" effort. The remainder or approximately half of the

Rice's farm became an extensive shopping area on the north side of Butterfield Road.

Each year more than ten thousand people enjoy the Danada Fall Festival. The one-day festival is usually held on the second Sunday in October. There you can see a variety of horse breed demonstrations, sit in saddles, color, build and name a cardboard hobby horse, take a hay wagon ride drawn by draft horses or a vintage tractor, paint pumpkins, jump around in a pen filled with golden straw, listen to blue grass music, eat food and drink cider and view nature art and photos in the Danada House. The most unique activity at the Danada Fall Festival is sponsored by the forest preserve's arborists who give children in tree saddles a tow with their tree climbing ropes into the canopy of large hundred year-old landmark burr oak trees. The kids love it and most of the festival's activities are free.

The Danada Equestrian Center offers many activities for horse lovers. Young horse lovers twelve years old and older can register for the "Horse Sense Summer Camp". Summer campers are taught about the care and feeding of horses from the ground up. Youngsters, feed, curry, pick horse hooves and learn about tack before getting in the saddle or taking a horse drawn wagon ride. Volunteers are needed to care for the horses and perform stable chores on a daily basis. There is a formula by which volunteers can earn and pay for their lesson time in the saddle. Once horse enthusiasts complete all of the equestrian lessons offered, packages of trail rides can be purchased.

Groups wanting an alternative to a bowling or miniature golf outing can enjoy a hayride and bonfire. The wagon rides travel past the Danada Prairie and near a heron rookery. It is not uncommon to see a great-horned owl, coyote and lots of herons and egrets coming and going at this wonderful mixture of horse heaven and nature's glory.

If you want to learn how to ride and care for a horse or enjoy a horse-drawn hayride with friends contact the Danada Equestrian Center at (630) 668-6012.

The Danada House is a great place to reserve for a party, wedding or other catered function. The addition, named the Atrium has a great dance floor and will hold a group of 150 persons. The Atrium's architecture includes lots of large glass windows connecting partygoers to the beautiful outdoor setting where it is possible to watch a fox trot inside or outside! For information or a Danada House tour you can call (630) 668-5392 or visit www.danadahouse.com.

TRAIL TALK

Today the support group named the "Friends of Danada" includes several of the original activists that were responsible for saving this historical, cultural and natural and living trophy. The Friends of Danada sponsors many activities and events that are held each year at the Danada Equestrian

Center, Danada House and farm. The Wild Horse Project is one of the most interesting programs sponsored by the friends group.

Prior to the start of this project the equestrian center relied on donated horses for use in their riding programs. Many of the horses were older senior steeds with lameness or other physical ailments. Horses in the stable's fleet were thoroughbreds and jumpers that were not entirely dependable throughout the weeks of beginner and intermediate riding courses. In 1998, the Wild Horse Project began as a solution to the dilemmas of having several horses needing medical rest and relaxation.

Wild mustang descendants of the horses brought to the Americas by Spanish conquistadors were adopted from western rangelands where their numbers are expanding and the natural resources are being diminished from wild horse and burro herds overgrazing. For the past eight years the Friends of Danada, a support group of the forest preserve has sponsored the adoption of mustangs. The training staff and volunteers and staff began a humane gentling program that is pretty much the opposite approach to the "busting bronco" rodeo style.

The horse-gentling program has worked out extremely well and today ten mustangs are part of the Danada's herd. The mustangs tend to be sturdy, versatile and strong without the lameness issues of the older horses retired from the racetrack or jumping competitions and then donated to the stable operation. It takes time for the staff and volunteers to train and prepare a wild horse so that a beginner horseman can ride. The time it takes to gentle and train the horses provides many learning for trainers, volunteers, staff members and visitors. It also provides lifetime protection for the horses and assists with the long-term management of western rangelands.

Herrick Lake and Danada forest preserves have wetlands that have been created from an intricate drainage system that flows from nearby subdivisions. Many species of dragonflies are darting over the marshes and high in the nearby cottonwood trees there is a colonial nesting site called a heron rookery. Great blue herons glide overhead from early spring through summer. It's busy as an airport as they come and go building rudimentary stick nests and then caring for nestlings. In winter a great-horned owl will nest in one of the vacated rookery nests.

In the spring riding past these wet areas can be loud with the sound of frog calls or songs. Volunteer frog monitors receive training from forest preserve staff to identify various frog species by listening to recordings of frog calls. After training volunteer frog monitors make frequent visits to wetlands and log data about the amphibians and attempt to verify the frog species that croak and sing. Spring peepers, Cope's tree frog, bullfrogs and American toads are just a few species recorded.

FOR MORE INFORMATION

Visit the Forest Preserve District of DuPage County website at www.dupageforest.com or telephone (630) 933-7200.

Fermi National Accelrator Laboratory Trail

5

BATAVIA / WARRENVILLE

TRAIL LENGTH

Fermilab has approximately thirty miles of roads, trails and pathways.

TRAIL SURFACE

Asphalt.

LOCATION

Bicyclists and trail users can enter Fermilab from Warrenville on the east side or Batavia from the west side.

From the east use the entrance located on Batavia Road west of Illinois Route 59 in Warrenville. From the west use the Pine Street entrance east of Kirk Road in Batavia.

TRAILHEAD LOCATIONS

A very small parking lot that often fills to capacity is located on the north side of Batavia Road at the east entrance in Warrenville. Near Batavia adequate parking is available at the education and visitor center parking lot near the west entrance east of Pine Street and Kirk Road.

TRAIL DESCRIPTION

Fermi National Accelerator Laboratory straddles western DuPage and eastern Kane Counties It is operated by the U.S. Department of Energy. Fermilab is a beautiful and safe place to ride a bike or in-line skate because there is not much traffic on the road system. The wind can be gutsy and gusty out there.

Many riders choose to travel through Fermi and reconnect with the Illinois Prairie Path. Bikers exiting west at Pine Street can turn south on the sidewalk on the west side of Kirk Road and within one mile reunite with the Batavia Illinois Prairie Path spur trail. Riders pedaling east can parallel Batavia Road on a ten-foot wide pathway and reunite with the Illinois Prairie Path east of the Batavia Road and Butterfield Road intersection in Warrenville.

TRAVELER'S NOTEBOOK

Trail users and bicyclists may enter the lab from 6 A.M. to 8 P.M. every day of the week. The lab has been closed to visitors when there is an elevated code orange terrorist alert.

There are about a hundred good reasons to pedal, hike or roll into Fermilab. There is always something interesting going on there. There are huge concrete basins and tunnels being constructed, there is fishing, huge bison with calves, heron rookeries, white-tailed deer, fawns, coyote, beaver, cooper's hawks and more songbirds than you can shake a stick at.

Other neat stuff about Fermi includes the few hills and views of wide-open midwest landscape. There are old barns, pastures, oak savannas, prairie, corn, hay and soybean fields, and wetlands. Near the entrance to Wilson Building the row of international flags and sculptured landscape, reflection pools and silver sculpted spires in the ponds gives the laboratory an international, artistic flare.

The scientists don't just stay in the buildings at the lab, there is a ton of research, education and restoration going on at the oak woodlots and prairies. The Lederman Science Center is very kid and family friendly. Besides the interactive exhibits a visit to the science center offers a science lab, a technology lab and a teacher resource center.

In addition, the lab advertises that it offers thirty-seven programs to families, teachers, students and researchers from kindergarten to postgraduate levels. Fermi's Website states that program topics vary. Hands-on programs guide participants to make discoveries and learn about physical science, mathematics, life science, engineering, earth and space science and technology. The list of the program titles is intriguing. Consider the fun you will have attending programs titled, *From Quarks to Quasars*, *Ask-a-Scientist*, *Beauty and Charm at Fermilab*, *Phriendly Physics*, *Particles and Prairies* or the *Cryogenic Show*.

The education center is open to the public Monday through Friday from 8:30 a.m. until 4:30 p.m. and on Saturdays from 9 a.m. to 3 p.m. Holiday hours vary and it is best to call ahead. Larger groups of five or more are requested to book a visit, Call (630) 840-8258 for more information.

Due in a great part to the lab's preservation and restoration efforts, there is great seasonal natural beauty. Woodland wildflowers cover the forest floor during the spring and early summer. There are white trout lilies, gold colored marsh marigolds, lavender wild geraniums and the laughing calls of yellow-shafted flickers in the woods. Later in the summer you can be immersed in the magnificence of a prairie, absorb its vast sea of multi-colored waves of grass and flowers. Nodding wild onion, Indian and big bluestem grass, prairie milkweed, tall coreopsis, Joe pye weed and prairie dock are just a few of the prairie plants present. Fermilab's prairie is expansive and it is absolutely loaded with many different types of colorful butterflies, noisy chirping crickets, grasshoppers, cicadas and locusts.

This is a great place to hit the wall, bonk and then simmer down and recover because it has so much nature and wildlife to soothe a weary body. Take some time off your bike and just look around this place. Better yet, pull up a piece of shade and take a load off and just listen to the vocalizations of nature's musicians. You'll be better for it.

TRAIL TALK

The ride that a partner and I took during an August evening told us that summer was definitely on the wane. The shadows were long, there were cool pockets in the low dips where we rode and I could hear cicadas and crickets. They rub their legs together to create that chirp and the cicada have thymbals to make the noise that reverberates through the woods.

The buffalo herd was close to the fence that night. In the olden days, during the Seventies, there was a sign hung on the fence that read, "Don't even think about crossing this field unless you run the hundred in seven seconds flat. The Bull can do it in eight." It is a good idea to show respect for animals as big and fast as the American bison.

We rode behind another rider thinking we might eventually wear him or her out and then pass by on the left. It never happened. We lost distance all the time as the rider bolted ahead gaining ground. It was fun to try to stay with another rider and chase them around Fermilab. Upon checking the odometer it made for a quick ten miles on the odometer. We ended up riding about twenty-three miles and never rode the same route at all.

Another ride in July provided us with a sunrise miracle. The ground fog rose in such a way that it raised like a four foot thick blanket and wavered up and down in the golden morning sunshine. We pedaled across and through this blanket sometimes with our heads and shoulders above the steamy sheet and other times tucked inside its yellow glow. We looked out over the fields as this sunlit fog blanket shifted and lofted. It will probably be a long time coming before there will be another sunrise gift that offers as much unusual natural beauty for the eyes. We were glad we got up early for that ride.

FOR MORE INFORMATION

Visit the Fermi National Accelerator Laboratory website at www.fnal.gov or telephone (630) 840-3000.

Fullersburg Woods Forest Preserve Trail

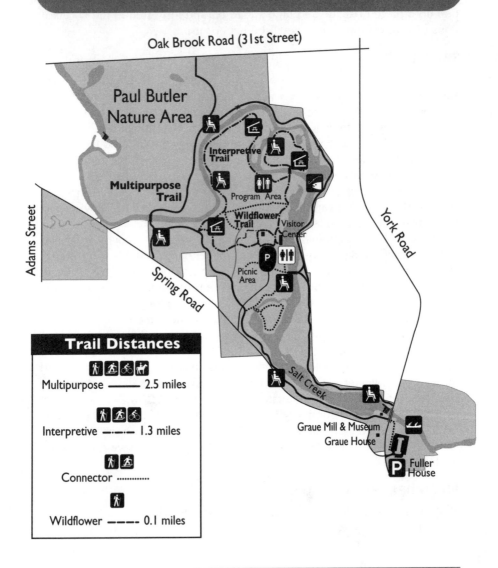

Oak Brook Road (31st Street)

Paul Butler
Nature Area

Adams Street

Interpretive
Trail

Multipurpose
Trail

Program Area

Wildflower
Trail

Visitor
Center

Spring Road

P

Picnic
Area

York Road

Salt Creek

Graue Mill & Museum
Graue House

Fuller
House

P

Trail Distances

Multipurpose ——— 2.5 miles

Interpretive —·—·— 1.3 miles

Connector ············

Wildflower —·—·— 0.1 miles

Fullersburg Woods Forest Preserve Trail

6

OAK BROOK

TRAIL LENGTH

A 2.5-mile loop trail along Salt Creek encircles Fullersburg Woods and connects to the Oak Brook Pathway. The second trail is a 1.3-mile loop interpretive trail that is part of the Fullersburg Woods Nature Center.

TRAIL SURFACE

Crushed limestone.

The Fullersburg Woods trails are groomed for diagonal and skate style cross-country skiing when there is adequate snow cover.

LOCATION

Fullersburg Woods is in Oak Brook on Spring Road, one-half mile south of 31st Street. From this direction there are rush hour turning restrictions and the road is temporarily closed during weekday mornings and afternoons to prevent drive thru traffic.

From the intersection of Ogden Avenue (U.S. Route 34) and York Road, take York Road north about two blocks to Spring Road. Turn left and take the curvy Spring Road to the Fullersburg Woods entrance on the right side. The address is 3609 Spring Road in Oak Brook.

TRAILHEAD LOCATIONS

Both trails are easily accessed from the Fullersburg Woods parking lot on Spring Road, one-half mile south of 31st Street and one-half mile northwest from the intersection of York Road and Ogden Avenue (U.S. Route 34). There are parking lots across from Graue Mill House and Museum along Spring Road and York Road.

TRAIL DESCRIPTION

The trails follow along both sides of Salt Creek and extend over mostly flat floodplain terrain, encircling Fullersburg Woods Forest preserve and passing by Fullersburg Woods Education Center, the historic Graue Mill, dam and York Tavern.

The trails provide visitors with the opportunity to see various waterfowl, beaver and other critters that make their home in Salt Creek or along the water's edge. The historic York Tavern cooks a good-tasting burger and the beer is always cold for a hungry and thirsty trail traveler. The Graue Mill, house and museum are one-of-a-kind historic spots.

Several picnic shelters and flat and arching bridges span Salt Creek. They were built with locally quarried limestone and large white oak trees felled by Civilian Conservation Corps during the late 1920s and early 1930s. The bridges and shelters are still in use and good repair.

The 1.3-mile interpretive trail offers self-guided tours that offer intriguing information about DuPage County's natural history. There is short steep hill that climbs past the restored prairie and Riverbend shelter. Bicyclists must be cautious since there are many children, nature watchers and walkers who use the interpretive trail for its educational purpose.

> **Bicycle riders should ride slowly and under strict control at all times along this trail.**

TRAVELER'S NOTEBOOK

One of the oldest forest preserves in DuPage County's system the 222-acre Fullersburg Woods Forest Preserve has been open to the public since 1928. Various educational programs are offered year around at the Nature Center.

Many family-oriented programs and activities make the trails highly rated for youngsters and beginning riders. The two most popular programs are the Earth Day event held the first Sunday after April 22 (Earth Day) and the award-winning Halloween Walks held on one of the last weekends in October.

At the Earth Day event, forest preserve arborists hoist youngsters clad in tree-climbing equipment into the oak tree's canopy and kids can hone their skills as forest firefighters taking aim at targets with portable water pumps. The Halloween Walks capitalize on the woods as the perfect setting for true, creepy nature stories. Along the dimly lit nature trails, families meet Fun Gus, the large talking mushroom that can rap about rap, rot and decay.

Many of this historic forest preserve's trail bridges and picnic shelters were built during the Depression era by the Civilian Conservation Corps. Salt Creek was dredged and small islands were also formed at this forest preserve while the CCC camp was here during the 1930s.

Seasonal blooms of many springtime woodland wildflowers can be seen during April and May. A picnic area with a non-reservable shelter is available west of the parking lot. Campfires, charcoal grills and alcohol are prohibited.

Fullersburg Woods is open daily. The entry gates at all DuPage County Forest Preserves are open one hour after sunrise and close one hour after sunset. The Visitor Center is open daily from 9 a.m. to 5 p.m. except on the Fourth of July, Thanksgiving and the day after, Christmas Eve, Christmas Day, Easter and New Year's Day. Call (630) 850-8110 for information.

Graue Mill is approximately one-half mile downstream from Fullersburg Woods Nature Center. Along the pathway to the mill, trekkers can stop to read signs that mark the location of the Salt Creek ice house, Ben Fuller residence and read highlights about the area's cultural history.

The three-story mill was built over a five-year period by Frederick Graue and was completed in 1852. According to *The DuPage County Guide*, "The bricks were made of clay from Graue's farm and burned in a kiln near the site. Stone for the foundation and trim was hauled from the Lemont limestone quarry, twelve miles northeast of Fullersburg. White oak for the posts, girders and joists was cut from a rich timber tract along the canal near Lemont. Construction was a triumph of pioneer craftsmanship."

During the Civil War era it was used as a safe house along the underground slave railroad. Today thousands of paying visitors come to see the National Registered Historic landmark. Costumed interpreters operate the mill and demonstrate how corn was ground into cornmeal. Other types of whole and ground grains are shown and it appears much different than when seen in a cereal bowl.

The large grinding circles of stone are now powered by an electric motor, and not by water shot through a millrace under the mill's water wheel. It is still an impressive sight to see and hear the huge round stones grind and ground the corn into fine cornmeal that can be purchased in authentic-looking cotton grain sacks. Recipes for cornbread and other cornmeal delights are available from the miller.

Graue Mill is located at York and Spring Road in Oak Brook and is open every day from 10 a.m. to 4:30 p.m., from mid-April to mid-November. For information about admission fees, programs or field trips contact the Graue Mill Museum at (630) 655-2090 or www.grauemill.org.

TRAIL TALK

Anyone who has camped out or spent time riding and hiking in woodlands begins to develop a fondness for all the life they contain. Day or night, cold or wet, hot or humid, woodlands are always a lively place and the more this is understood, the bigger and more diverse a woodland grows. We come to know and understand some of its living organisms very well. Some of us know how to identify the woodland bird species, where they nest and when they migrate, their song, how many eggs are usually in a clutch and when they fledge. Others of us know about other species of insects and plants, while many of us just treasure the woodland for its tranquility and solitude, sunrises and sunsets.

The remaining woodlands in DuPage County must be preserved forever. In the recent past, lack of a fire regime caused most areas to change into dense growths of Eurasian shrubs. The shrubs that shaded the ground threatened native species of woodland plants like red and white flowered trillium, bloodroot, hepatica, spring beauty, Virginia waterleaf and many others. The woodland varieties of both plant and animal species waned and have had limitations to diversity and range. Plants that followed and seeded in behind the settlers, and advances in agriculture and technology supplanted native species of flora and fauna.

Fullersburg Woods Forest Preserve is a native oak forest remnant that remains. If the woodlands are to remain as established functioning ecosystems for future generations they must receive natural area triage that is managed and prescribed by humans. It is a serious challenge to maintain high quality woodlands in a biologically diverse condition for the benefit of all living things.

FOR MORE INFORMATION

Visit the Forest Preserve District of DuPage County's website at www.dupageforest.com or telephone (630) 933-7200. Contact Graue Mill and Museum at (630) 655-2090 or www.grauemill.org.

Photo courtesy of Dick Todd.

Great Western Trail in DuPage County

7

TRAIL LENGTH

11.4 miles

Trail Surface

Crushed limestone.

Location

The eastern terminus of the Great Western Trail is in Villa Park just one block north of the Illinois Prairie Path at Villa Avenue. The western trailhead is located slightly north of Kline Creek Farm near Prince Crossing Road where it joins the Illinois Prairie Path in Timber Ridge Forest Preserve in Winfield.

Trailhead Locations

Parking for the Great Western Trail is available along Villa Avenue in downtown Villa Park. There is a small parking area at Churchill Woods Forest Preserve located one-quarter mile north of St. Charles Road on the east side of Swift Road in Glen Ellyn. At the west end of the Great Western Trail parking is available at Kline Creek Farm located on the west side of County Farm Road approximately one-quarter mile south of the trail in Winfield. There is also a small parking lot on the east side of Prince Crossing Road south of St. Charles Road and north of Geneva Road. This lot is within a stone's throw of the Elgin Spur of the Illinois Prairie Path.

Trail Description

The trail is mostly flat and constructed of limestone screenings maintained by the DuPage Department of Transportation. There are flush restroom facilities with a drinking fountain at Kline Creek Farm and at the eastern terminus in Villa Park. The trail is within one block of connecting to the Illinois Prairie Path at Villa Avenue in Villa Park. Streetlights have been installed along the Great Western Trail in Villa Park.

With the exception of the bridge over the Interstate 355 tollway, most road crossings are unprotected for hikers and bikers. One must be a wary traveler. The electrical power towers that line the trail make it an uninspiring route and a bit noisy. Overhead buzzing lines are easily heard and they can be annoying.

In spite of its lack of amenities and aesthetics, the Great Western Trail is a smooth ride and is well maintained. Several parks along the route offer scenic and recreational diversions. The trail is less traveled than the Illinois Prairie Path and is a good connection to the west side of DuPage County from east side cities and villages. At its western terminus the rider or hiker continues along the Illinois Prairie Path Elgin Spur.

TRAVELER'S NOTEBOOK

Eventually the Great Western Trail connects with and joins the Elgin Spur of the Illinois Prairie Path. There is a scenic 5.9-mile triangular route that can be traveled by taking the Great Western Trail west from County Farm Road to Prince Crossing Road. A after traveling a short distance south (approximately .1 mile) a trail user can merge into the Illinois Prairie Path's Elgin Spur and travel east thru Timber Ridge Forest Preserve to the intersection of Geneva Road and County Farm Road in Winfield. A connector trail from the Illinois Prairie Path and Great Western Trail extends to Kline Creek Farm Visitor Center and Parking lot before joining the Great Western Trail.

TRAIL TALK

This is a rails-to-trails conversion that was built and opened in 1992 on the abandoned main line of the Chicago Great Western Railroad. The track was constructed in 1886 to 1887. The former Great Western Railroad Depot in Villa Park was built in 1926 and is a scenic amenity last used by the Villa Park Men's Garden Club. The trail offers a great connector to the western edge of DuPage County, the Illinois Prairie Path, several forest preserve trails and scenic points of interest beyond.

According to former DuPage County Board Chairman Jack Knuepfer, the idea to purchase the Great Western Trail corridor "was an idea that was supported wholeheartedly and there was never a doubt about its success'. The notion was to provide it as a recreational trail using it as a successful link to connect many forest preserves."

When asked if he has been surprised by the trail's popularity Mr. Knuepfer said, "Not at all. I think all the trails in DuPage County supplied a need we had in DuPage County. I think the trail system passes public muster. It's a traffic problem on some weekends and we need all the width we can get. Phil Elfstrom (former Kane County Board Chairman and champion for the Fox River Trail) and I envisioned a trail going into the other five collar counties (Lake, Kane, Will, McHenry and DuPage)."

FOR MORE INFORMATION

Contact DuPage Department of Transportation at (630) 407-6883 or visit www.dupageco.org/bikeways.

BIKING RELEASES THE CHILD

Reporter John Leicester provided a look into six-time Tour de France champion Lance Armstrong, and he also describes the youthful feelings we all have had tingling through our systems while biking.

"He (Lance) joked and chatted with teammates who wore special blue jerseys with yellow stripes. They stretched in a line across the road with their leader for motorcycle-riding photographers to record the moment. The team was the muscle behind Armstrong's win, leading him in grueling mountain climbs, shielding him from crashes and wind, and keeping him stoked with drinks and food.

In 2003 Armstrong beat Ullrich by just 61 secondsæby far his narrowest victory. He now admits he was not in great shape.

'I paid the price and learned a valuable lesson, and I won't ever make that mistake again,' he said.

In 2004 he roared back with renewed fire.

'It's as if I was with my five friends and we were thirteen years old and we all had new bikes and we said, 'OK, we're going to race from here to there,' he said. 'You want to beat your friends more than anything. You're sprinting and you're attacking. It was like that for me. A simple pleasure.'"

Greene Valley Forest Preserve Trail

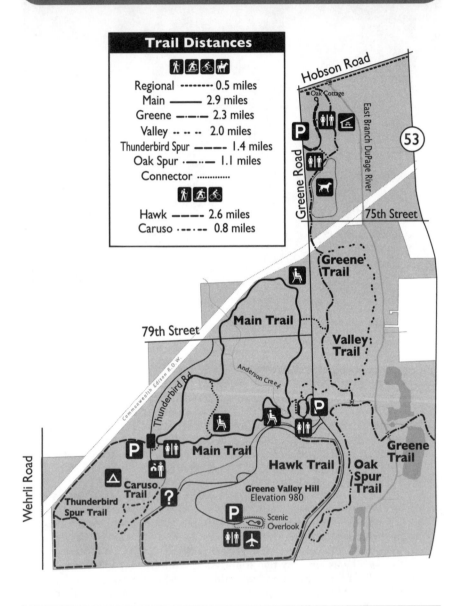

Trail Distances

Regional ------- 0.5 miles
Main ———— 2.9 miles
Greene —·—·— 2.3 miles
Valley ·· ·· ·· 2.0 miles
Thunderbird Spur ———— 1.4 miles
Oak Spur ·——··— 1.1 miles
Connector ············

Hawk ———— 2.6 miles
Caruso ·—··—· 0.8 miles

Hobson Road
Oak Cottage
Greene Road
East Branch DuPage River
53
75th Street
Greene Trail
Main Trail
Valley Trail
79th Street
Commonwealth Edison R.O.W.
Thunderbird Rd
Anderson Creek
Wehrli Road
Main Trail
Greene Trail
Caruso Trail
Hawk Trail
Oak Spur Trail
Thunderbird Spur Trail
Greene Valley Hill
Elevation 980
Scenic Overlook

Greene Valley Forest Preserve Trail

8

NAPERVILLE

TRAIL LENGTH

Seven miles of looped trails meander throughout the forest preserve. The Greene Valley trail is groomed for diagonal and skate style cross-country skiing when there is adequate snow cover.

TRAIL SURFACE

Crushed limestone.

LOCATION

Greene Valley is located in Naperville near 75th Street and Illinois Route 53 and has several parking options. The north area and parking lot is located on east side of Greene Road, 0.3 mile north of 75th Street and 0.3-mile south of Hobson Road. The Thunderbird Youth Camp is located on 79th Street, a half-mile west of Greene Road and the parking lot is near the end of a long and winding entrance drive. The south parking lot is located south of 79th Street, west of Greene Road.

TRAILHEAD LOCATIONS

For convenient access to primitive restrooms, water, picnic areas, reservable shelters and trails travel to the north parking area on the east side of Greene Road between 75th Street and Hobson offers the best access to the trails. If you are looking for an anaerobic work out and steep hill climb park at the base of the former landfill hill south of 75th and 79th Streets on the west side of Greene Road, Another trailhead parking lot is located near the Thunderbird Youth Camp at the end of a long entrance road south off of 79th Street.

TRAIL DESCRIPTION

Greene Valley Forest Preserve has 1,425 acres and features nearly ten miles of trails with a long, steep 190-foot tall hill to climb. This forest preserve is a popular destination for horseback riders and so bicyclists will need to use caution. Trails meander and slice through woodlands, meadows and a riverine ecosystem. There are some hilly sections, especially when coursing through the woodlots blind curves and when approaching Greene Road and 79th Street. There is an underpass that allows bicyclists and hikers safe passage under 75th Street near the East Branch of the DuPage River.

The former landfill site, now a scenic overlook, is now open on a limited basis to visitors. On weekends spring through fall many visitors enjoy the challenge of biking or hiking to the top of the 200-acre hill and standing 190 feet above the land surface, which is equivalent to 980 feet above sea level. On a clear day it offers a fantastic view of the Chicago skyline. Nature watchers will enjoy watching sandill cranes, geese, ducks, hawks and eagles migrating in the spring and fall. It is also a great spot to see the spectacular fall colors of the surrounding oak woods. Be careful on the way downhill. Loose gravel is hazardous and would cause a terrible case of road rash. Be sure to call (630) 933-7248 to find out when the hill is accessible for a climb.

The Greene Valley trail connects to the on and off road Southern DuPage County Regional Trail that parallels 75th Street from the eastern to western edge of DuPage County.

TRAVELER'S NOTEBOOK

Rangers have sighted a bobcat at the south end of the trail system. The "wood ghost," as the bobcat is sometimes called, was spotted near the East Branch of the DuPage River at the edge of the oak woods called "Blessing Hill." The hill near southern boundary of Greene Valley is named "Blessing Hill" because it is the former site where foxhounds, horses and red-jacketed equestrians received a reverend's blessing before the start of the foxhunt.

Animal ecologists from the DuPage County Forest Preserve District placed a tracking box in the area. This had a Q-tip soaked in bobcat urine standing upright in the sand of the tracking box. Bobcat track impressions were later recorded in the moist sand. Since bobcats are very secretive animals you will be considered lucky if you were ever to catch a glimpse of one. That is why "wood ghost" is such an appropriate nickname for the bobcat.

The wooded areas at Greene Valley provide a spectacular display of wildflowers in late April and May. The forest floor is definitely carpeted with columbine, wild geranium, trout lily and bloodroot. Management such as burning and selective tree removal allows more light into the dense forest areas and creates a more open condition that favors growth for the native plants. Hikers may identify morel mushrooms and bladderwort shrubs in the wooded area known as Hinterlong Bird Sanctuary north of 79th Street.

Invasive brush and tree removal has begun to revitalize the habitat for songbirds and other wildlife at Greene Valley Forest Preserve. The thirty-acre community of young small trees and shrubs is a favored habitat for many songbirds. The trailside area near the river has been replanted with native shrubs such as wild plum, Iowa crab Allegheny shadblow and native willows. In time this area will provide nesting sites and beneficial habitat for butterflies and insects that support other shrubland residents like the yellow-breasted chat, blue-winged warbler, orchard oriole and yellow-billed cuckoo.

TRAIL TALK

Even though Greene Valley Forest Preserve is in a green valley it is named after its historic owners and area early settlers, the Greene family, not a green valley. This preserve's history has an agricultural past similar to many forest preserve areas of DuPage County. In 1835, William Briggs Greene purchased 200 acres of land from Daniel Greene, his uncle. When the land was surveyed in 1840 those who mapped it stated they ". . . left Brill's wheat field and entered hazel and red oak brush and scattering timber." This type of description of scattered and stunted oak trees interspersed with thorn thickets and wooded ravines give today's visitors an idea of how the area once looked. In 1841, William Greene built the first section of Oak Cottage, a farmhouse that stands today on the southeast corner of Greene and Hobson roads.

In his book of memoirs titled *God Bless Our House* William Bertram Greene described his father's first bicycle experience sometime during the late 1800s:

"When I was five, one of the hired men had a high-wheel bicycle. Its seat and center of gravity were almost over the high wheel so that a fairly small stone could block the big wheel while the rider would keep on going (over the handlebars). Father undertook to learn to ride one evening after supper. He was thrown headfirst in the traditional manner ending up with a badly sprained arm, black and blue, and laid up for about a month. The very modern and cocky young doctor (Dr. W.J. Truitt) had a new contraption—a galvanic battery machine; it supplied mechanical vibration along with electrical stimulation. Father got well."

FOR MORE INFORMATION

Visit the Forest Preserve District of DuPage County website at www.dupageforest.com or telephone (630) 933-7200.

ALWAYS AVOID DEHYDRATION

- Bring lots of water
- Drink early and often. Fluid loss or dehydration can occur quickly when exercising outdoors.
- Bring sports drinks when you will be out for a long time (two hours or more) these beverages replace important fluids and contain potassium, sodium and carbohydrates that move to the muscle during exercise providing energy endurance on a long trip.

Herrick Lake Forest Preserve Trail

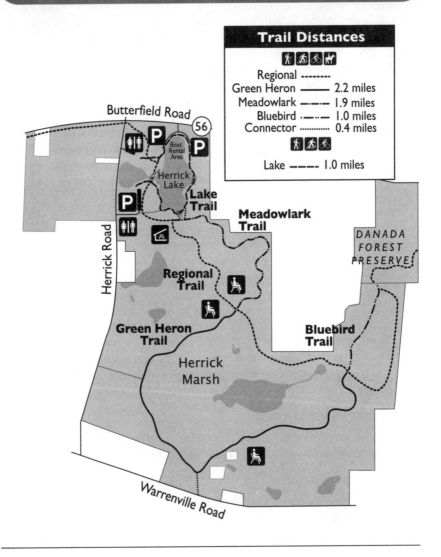

Trail Distances

Regional ·········
Green Heron ———— 2.2 miles
Meadowlark —·—·— 1.9 miles
Bluebird ·—·—·— 1.0 miles
Connector ············ 0.4 miles

Lake ———— 1.0 miles

Butterfield Road

56

Boat Rental Area

Herrick Lake

Lake Trail

Meadowlark Trail

Herrick Road

DANADA FOREST PRESERVE

Regional Trail

Green Heron Trail

Bluebird Trail

Herrick Marsh

Warrenville Road

Herrick Lake
Forest Preserve Trail

9

WHEATON

TRAIL LENGTH

Herrick Lake has 6.5 miles of looped trails.

TRAIL SURFACE

Crushed limestone.

The Herrick Lake Trail is groomed for diagonal and skate style cross-country skiing when there is adequate snow cover. Trails connect to other well-groomed cross-country ski trails at Arrowhead Golf Course.

LOCATION

In Wheaton, the main entrance is located on the south side of Butterfield Road (Illinois Route 56) approximately one mile west of Naperville Road. The south parking lot is located on the east side of Herrick Road, one-quarter mile south of Butterfield Road.

TRAILHEAD LOCATIONS

There are two parking lots that offer easy access to trails at Herrick Lake Forest Preserve in Wheaton. The entrance closest to the concession area, flush toilets and picnic areas is located on south side of Butterfield Road (Illinois Route 56). Another smaller lot is located on the east side of Herrick Road. This lot is close to primitive toilets and a hand pump.

TRAIL DESCRIPTION

The Herrick Lake trail system is one of two trail projects that have been designated as National Recreation Trails. The national recreational trail designation is awarded by the National Park Service to exemplary trails of local and regional significance, and the designated trails are featured as part of America's national system of trails. Several marked looped trails and trail connections make the Herrick Lake trail system perfect for any length of time that a person has for a jaunt.

Herrick Lake has a "Lake Trail" that is one-mile long, pancake-flat and encircles the lake. People with strollers, walkers and small children frequently use this trail. It offers good views of the lake and picnic areas and is probably the most popular and most traveled section of trail in this forest preserve. From there, marked trails cut through central and southern parts of the preserve.

The Herrick Lake trails link up with the Danada Forest Preserve trails to the east. There is an approximate one-mile path segment that extends west and parallels Butterfield Road and links the Herrick Lake trails with both the Blackwell Forest Preserve trail and the Illinois Prairie Path near Warrenville Grove Forest Preserve.

In the winter when enough snow has fallen, trails are groomed for classical and skate-style cross-country skiing. The trails offer some access to additional cross-country skiing at Wheaton Park District's Arrowhead Golf Course. When open and groomed the trails at Arrowhead Golf Course offer some of the best cross-country ski trails in Chicagoland. Ski equipment is available for rent at the banquet facility. There are gentle and steep hills on the course that provide challenge and interesting terrain to beginner, intermediate and expert skinny skiers. Many cross-country skiers gather at Arrowhead for the annual Nordic Fox ski race (approximately twelve kilometers) held in late January. Many skiers also train for the American Birkebeiner, America's premier cross-country ski marathon (held annually in northern Wisconsin) at Arrowhead and Herrick Lake Forest Preserve.

TRAVELER'S NOTEBOOK

Herrick Lake is one of the most visited forest preserves in the DuPage County system. It offers an array of recreational facilities for the outdoors person and a variety of ecosystems for the naturalist.

The preserve has long been a favorite picnic spot and offers two shelters. The older and most popular shelter was built in the 1930s by the Civilian Conservation Corps and has a large flagstone fireplace. Be sure to bring your own firewood. The newer shelter is popular because of its proximity to flush toilets, food concession and boat rental area. Both shelters overlook the lake and are great places to picnic and take a break from the trails' challenges.

Reservations for the shelters and other picnic areas can be made through the District offices, by mail or by phone with a charge card by calling (630) 933-7248. If you plan to make a reservation call early these sites are popular and are often reserved within the first days of January each New Year.

Herrick Lake has been stocked often with several species of fish for the past thirty years. A free loaner fishing pole can be acquired from the concession area when it is staffed on summer days. Largemouth bass, channel and flathead catfish, crappie and sunfish provide angling fun from the shore and from rental canoes or rowboats. Private boats are not permitted. Fishermen 16 years of age or older, are required to have a fishing license.

In the 1980s the Hesterman Drain Project created a marsh and partially underground drainage system to relieve Wheaton neighborhoods from flooding. Eastern tiger salamanders, northern leopard frogs, pied-billed grebes, blue winged teal, mink, fox, coyote and muskrat live in this expansive wetland. Black ash and buttonbush make up some of the vegetative density along the preserve's glacial pothole marshes and flatland streams. The beauty of the wetlands provides a peaceful feeling for passersby and there are Lincoln log style benches that are situated near overlooks of wondrous and wet natural areas.

The oak woodlands contain some beautiful 150 year-old landmark trees. The woods have received lots of restoration work in recent years. Now that more sunlight reaches the forest floor spring woodland wild flowers abound during spring. The trail route extends past restored groves of white and burr oak trees south of the main picnic areas near the Hesterman marsh.

This is a good place to get off the bike or off the trail and explore. Indigo buntings, scarlet tanagers, bluebirds and goldfinches are just a few of the songbirds that can be spotted in this area. Once you are back on the trail you will see a long winding hill that takes winds through the woods and into the open area near the marsh. It is a great hill going down south and east and a challenging hill to push up curving to the top as you travel north and west.

TRAIL TALK

The original landowner of this area was Ira Herrick who moved from Vermont to the rich countryside approximately thirty miles west of Lake Michigan in 1832. Ira's grandson Frank Earl Herrick (born in 1875) wrote lots of poetry and was given the official title of Wheaton's poet laureate. There are volumes of his poetry at the DuPage County Historical Museum. A senior docent curator at the museum said that, "nary a leaf would fall and Frank E. Herrick would write a poem about the occasion." There are oodles of odes in the collection. There are poems that honor hundreds of local citizens, about many places and events in his life.

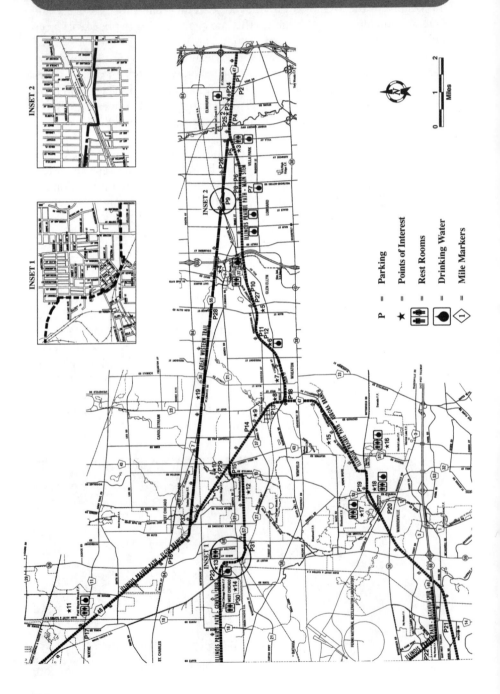

Illinois Prairie Path

TRAIL LENGTH

At 61 miles in length this Granddaddy of All Trails crosses from Cook County through DuPage County and enters eastern Kane County.

TRAIL SURFACE

Mostly crushed limestone with some short distances of asphalt.

LOCATION

The main stem of the Illinois Prairie Path has its eastern terminus at First Avenue in Maywood (Cook County). The path extends west fifteen miles west to Wheaton near Volunteer Park where it makes a major fork, branching in two directions.

The fourteen-mile northwesterly Elgin Branch connects to the Fox River Trail in Elgin. The second Illinois Prairie Path branch, the Aurora Branch, extends thirteen miles in a northeasterly direction and connects to the Fox River Trail at Aurora.

There are two segments, called spurs, which extend off the two main forks. The Geneva Spur splits off the Elgin Branch and extends eleven miles to connect with the Fox River Trail in Geneva. Another segment called the Batavia Spur splits off the Aurora Branch and extends six miles into Batavia and connects to the Fox River Trail.

In addition, a separate trail named the Great Western Trail angles from approximately one block north of the path's main stem near Villa Avenue in Villa Park. The Great Western Trail travels west for twelve miles and connects to the Prairie Path's Elgin Branch and Geneva Spur.

TRAILHEAD LOCATIONS

Parking and accessible points to the trail and spurs are located in every city and village the trail passes through, including Elmhurst, Villa Park, Lombard, Glen Ellyn, Wheaton, beautiful Warrenville, West Chicago, Winfield and Wayne.

The main fork and the two segments that branch to Aurora and Elgin can be accessed from the City of Wheaton's at Volunteer Park.

The Elgin Branch can be accessed from Timber Ridge Forest Preserve at Kline Creek Farm on the west side of County Farm Road in Winfield and near Pratt's Wayne Woods Forest Preserve on the north side of Army Trail Road in Wayne.

The Aurora Branch can be easily reached from Herrick Lake Forest Preserve parking lot on the south side of Butterfield Road (Illinois Route 56) in Wheaton, Blackwell Forest Preserve on the north side of Butterfield

Road (Illinois Route 56) in Warrenville or Warrenville Grove Forest Preserve parking area located on the northeast side Batavia Road in Warrenville. Be aware that Warrenville Grove's parking lot is small and does not have room for more than ten cars.

TRAIL DESCRIPTION

The Illinois Prairie Path has a lot to offer people of DuPage County. Each year it is used by more than 400,000 hikers, dog walkers, joggers, bikers, cross-country skiers, horseback riders, and other self-propelled outdoor adventurers. It is open every day of the year and there are no fees.

The trail is always well maintained by the DuPage Department of Transportation and gains maintenance assistance from a very active group of volunteers. At last count there were more than 2,000 volunteers involved with the stewardship of this recreational trail system! For more information on how to volunteer visit the Illinois Prairie Path's Web site at www.IPP.org or call (630) 681-2221.

There are mapped locations of restrooms and drinking fountains along the trail in The Illinois Prairie Path and The Great Western Trail guide available from the DuPage County Division of Transportation. To request a map, visit the DuPage County Division of Transportation Web site at www.dupageco.org/bikeways/index or telephone (630) 682-7318.

If you are comfort-minded and desire a flush toilet they can also be easily located in the towns and villages that the Illinois Prairie Path passes through. The trail passes through miles of open countryside as it splits and heads west from the Wheaton area toward Aurora and Elgin, so it is a good idea to take care of the necessities before heading west toward the Fox River. The trail is mostly flat but there are some long gentle inclines that can wear on you if you are pushing uphill or invigorate if you're breezing along with a tailwind headed downhill.

The wide-open areas can be very sunny and windy which makes for fun if there is a tailwind and you remembered the sun block. It can be a tussle if the wind is in your face and you are challenged by a long, steady incline such as the trail section heading east from the Fox River Valley toward Warrenville. What a grind! The crosswinds are usually okay to deal with and trail users can be protected from the wind and sun by shade-lending trees that bend and bow over the trail.

Additional mileage for a Century Ride or a 100-plus mile pedal can be added by taking the Fox River Trail north into McHenry County Prairie Trail and ending or turning around near Richmond. The Fox River trail has also been extended a good distance south thru Aurora and into Oswego or you can connect from the Fox River Trail in St. Charles to the Great Western Trail that runs west from LeRoy Oaks Forest Preserve in St. Charles to Sycamore.

RATE YOUR TRIP!

Wheaton to the Kline Creek Farm, an 1890s farm, is approximately 7 miles.

West from Wheaton to North Avenue roundtrip is about 12 miles.

Wheaton west to Geneva and back is approximately 23 miles.

Wheaton southwest to Aurora and back is approximately 28 miles.

Wheaton to Batavia and back is about 29 miles.

A triangle trip west from Wheaton to Geneva to Batavia and back to Wheaton is approximately 30 miles.

Heading west from Wheaton to Elgin and back is approximately 32 miles.

From Wheaton west to Batavia, south to Aurora and east to Wheaton is approximately 33 miles.

Wheaton west to Geneva, south to Aurora and east to Wheaton is another triangle trip of approximately 37 miles.

Wheaton west to Elgin, south to Batavia and back east into Wheaton is about 43 miles.

Wheaton to Elgin to Aurora and back to Wheaton triangle is approximately 48 miles.

TRAVELER'S NOTEBOOK

The Illinois Prairie Path was the first major railroad bed that converted to a trail system in the United States. It is located within the former right-of-way of the Chicago, Aurora & Elgin interurban through the western suburbs.

The trail was established through the enthusiastic efforts of noted naturalist and author May Theilgaard Watts. She was also the founder of the Illinois Prairie Path Corporation. In 1971 the Illinois Prairie Path was designated as a National Recreational Trail.

Many of the cities along the trail have taken beautification measures and planted native Illinois prairie plants. Purple coneflower, compass plant, black-eyed Susan and New England aster add a pristine beauty and attract many species of butterflies. During the height of summer it is not uncommon to see and hear the ruby-throated hummingbird hovering and humming near nectar producing flowers alongside the trail. Some of their favorite nectar-producing flowers include; columbine, trumpet vine, salvia and bee balm.

For casually touring cyclists the towns of Winfield, Wheaton, Glen Ellyn, Lombard, Villa Park and Elmhurst offer summer farmers markets, fine shopping, good eating and some ice cream-licking options along the way. Midwest Cyclery, 117 East Front Street in Wheaton (630) 668-2424 and Prairie Path Cycles, 27 West Geneva, Winfield (630) 690-9749 are in close proximity to the path and offer tires, tubes and bicycle repair. If the repairs aren't too involved and the shop isn't too busy the folks who work there can sometimes accomplish a fix while you wait.

As you travel further west toward the Fox River the landscape's scenery is natural and wild looking. The branch that extends to Elgin courses past Lincoln Marsh in Wheaton and through Timber Ridge Forest Preserve near Winfield and Pratt's Wayne Woods in Wayne. In my opinion, this segment is the most scenic and beautiful route.

As you ride you'll be elevated over several marshes and be able to watch painted and snapping turtles sunning themselves on moss-covered floating logs, red-tailed hawks and kestrels might float overhead or soar past at eye level. Pratt's Wayne Woods Forest Preserve is the largest expanse of habitat in DuPage County and glimpses of rare yellow-headed blackbirds or a brood of sandhill cranes are possible for the observant cyclist.

Kline Creek Farm, an 1890s living history farm near Winfield, is an entertaining destination. It is less than one-mile north in distance from the Illinois Prairie Path on a connector trail between the Illinois Prairie Path and the Great Western Trail. The farm has costumed interpreters in period dress and they are well informed and very willing to chat about what farm life was like in this neck of the woods (and fields) during the 1890s. The 200-acre working farm exhibits championship-bred stock of shorthorn cattle and Southdown sheep. Draft horses can be seen out in the fields plowing or harvesting and during special weekends horse drawn wagon rides are offered.

The Geneva Spur of the Illinois Prairie Path passes by the 305-acre West Chicago Prairie Forest Preserve in West Chicago, a beautiful prairie remnant and a most active restoration site. Thousands of volunteer hours have been spent working to increase and improve plant and animal habitats. The prairie has more than 530 native plant species recorded. Prescribed burns, selective removal of aggressive non-native plants, seed collection and redistribution of native species are all part of the adaptive management activities that have taken place here for more than twenty years. Since 1980 direct personal involvement has been the essence of this conservation effort. Each year the West Chicago Prairie Stewardship Group contributes thousands of hours of sweat equity because of their love of land.

TRAIL TALK

The Illinois Prairie Path has a lot to offer. The Batavia Spur is about six miles long and ends up in Kane County at the Fox River Trail that runs along the east side of the Fox River in Batavia. Early in the morning before sunrise the air was cool and as it got light out we saw a family of raccoons. The young juveniles were learning to fend for themselves and scurried away as we approached. With their curved arching backs they made me laugh as they took off into the thick brush lining the trail and I imagine hearing their high pitched chattering as I cruise past. Generally the young 'coons may stay with a parent over winter but do learn to hunt and fend for themselves after twelve to sixteen weeks.

Pratt's Wayne Woods Forest Preserve in Wayne lies next to the Elgin spur of the Illinois Prairie Path west of Winfield and West Chicago. Pratt's Wayne Woods is the largest forest preserve in DuPage County. Located in the county's northwest corner, the preserve's 3,432 acres combine with the Illinois Department of Natural Resources' land to its north to form a continuous 4,000-acre stretch of land, a scarce resource in a growing urban area.

Pratt's Wayne Woods' numerous wetlands provide a lush environment for waterfowl including egrets, great blue herons, wood ducks, state-threatened sandhill cranes and state-endangered yellow-headed blackbirds, for which the preserve was designated as an Important Bird Area. Its prairies also host habitat for red-tailed hawks, screech owls and the state-threatened Henslow's sparrow.

FOR MORE INFORMATION

Visit the Illinois Prairie Path Website at www.IPP.org or www.dupageco.org/bikeways/index or telephone (630) 681-2221. To receive a trail map call (630) 682-7318.

MAKE A DIFFERENCE!

Act locally: join the Illinois Prairie Path organization. The Illinois Prairie Path group hosts trail rides, and conducts trail cleanups and a wide range of positive civic improvements. It's a great way to make a difference in the community. Check www.IPP.org to find out more and to become a member.

Mallard Lake Forest Preserve Trail

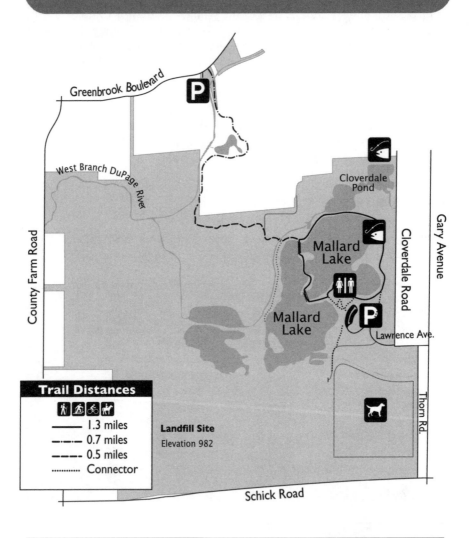

Trail Distances

————			1.3 miles
—·—·—			0.7 miles
— — —			0.5 miles
·············			Connector

Greenbrook Boulevard

West Branch DuPage River

County Farm Road

Cloverdale Pond

Mallard Lake

Mallard Lake

Gary Avenue

Cloverdale Road

Lawrence Ave.

Thorn Rd.

Landfill Site
Elevation 982

Schick Road

Mallard Lake
Forest Preserve Trail

10

HANOVER PARK

TRAIL LENGTH

A looped 2.3-mile trail from the parking lot west of Lawrence Avenue leads bikers and hikers through Mallard Lake's scenic picnic area and across the lake via two bridges.

TRAIL SURFACE

Crushed limestone.

LOCATION

Mallard Lake Forest Preserve is in Hanover Park. It is located on Lawrence Avenue, just west of Gary Avenue and north of Schick Road. Travel north on Gary Avenue to Lawrence Avenue, and continue west on Lawrence Avenue to the Mallard Lake Forest Preserve entrance. There is also a new entrance on the north side of Schick Road at a stoplight west of Gary Avenue.

TRAILHEAD LOCATIONS

The parking area and best location for trail access is in the main parking lot that is located west of Lawrence Avenue and north of Schick Road.

TRAIL DESCRIPTION

The trail at the 949-acre Mallard Lake Forest Preserve winds through and over a mixture of habitats including a large eighty-acre lake, grassy meadows and scattered woodlands. The 2.3-mile trail leads visitors through the preserve's picnic area which has a water pump and primitive-style latrines. This beautiful near the base of a former landfill trail passes over relatively flat terrain and two bridges that span narrow parts of the lake. The hill is closed to the public at the present time.

The Mallard Lake trail is accessible from the Bartlett Bike Paths and Hanover Park Bike Route. These communities' pathways connect and enter the northern border of Mallard Lake from Greenbrook Boulevard. The trail will extend west into Hawk Hollow Forest Preserve and a bridge will span across County Farm Road to complete the connection.

Miles of trails can be pedaled by joining the smooth and nicely laid out Bartlett Bike Path. Everyday the possibilities are endless for fishing, hiking, picnicking, bird watching, swimming, shooting hoops, playing field sports, shopping or dining. There are more than twenty miles of interconnected paths and trails in this neck of the woods. Since they are all off-road, they are very family friendly.

TRAVELER'S NOTEBOOK

Mallard Lake is a great place to fish or bird watch. The eighty-five acre lake has been stocked with largemouth bass, flathead catfish, channel catfish, crappie, northern pike and bluegill. Because of the lake's size there are great opportunities for viewing many species of waterfowl and shorebirds. It is a good idea to pack a pair of binoculars when you visit this preserve's trails. Autumn stopovers by gadwall, pintail, blue-winged teal and migrating Canada geese are common sights. During the summer, kingfishers, green herons, great blue herons and white egrets can be seen along the shoreline along with the ranks of fishermen.

The Mallard Lake trail is part of the North Central DuPage County Regional Trail. Forest preserve trails and community bike routes on and off roads extend through Wood Dale, Itasca, Spring Creek Reservoir and Meacham Grove forest preserves in Bloomingdale, Hanover Park, Bartlett and Mallard Lake Forest Preserve. The West DuPage Regional Trail will eventually connect with the North Central County Regional Trail and continue into the West Branch Forest Preserve in Bartlett and follow the West Branch of the DuPage River south. This trail will have few road crossings and includes more than twenty miles of continuous forest preserve trails.

Once complete, the West DuPage Regional Trail will be a valuable resource to be enjoyed by hikers, bikers, equestrians and cross-country skiers. More than ninety percent of the trail will be on forest preserve land. It will connect trail travelers with a wide variety of recreational areas and facilities including twelve forest preserves, sixteen local parks, five National Historic Register sites and many other points of interest from north to south.

TRAIL TALK

Despite of the fact that 217 acres of Mallard Lake served as a landfill from 1975 to 1999, wild things still abound. There are 262 native plant species, 115 different kinds of fish, amphibians, reptiles, birds and mammals to see and appreciate. The two fishing lakes, eighty-five acre Mallard Lake and seven-acre Cloverdale Pond offer alluring chances to catch and release trophy-sized fish.

Keep your eyes to the skies or water and you might observe wood ducks, pintail ducks, common mergansers, ruddy ducks, cormorants or kestrels. In early spring common loons are often seen on DuPage County lakes but it is a rare exception if a loon's mournful call is heard by visitors.

The Mallard Lake Forest Preserve includes a fifty person reservable shelter, drinking well, primitive restrooms, a dog exercise area and two easily accessible fishing piers. As time goes on the preserve will add several facilities. A scenic overlook, archery range, interpretive birdwatchers blind, carry-in boat launching area, winter sports area and more trails are just a few of the recreational components being considered for this forest preserve.

FOR MORE INFORMATION

Visit the Forest Preserve District of DuPage County website at www.dupageforest.com or telephone (630) 933-7200.

TRY A DIFFERENT TAKE!

Try cycling a trail during off-peak hours—early morning, late evening under a full moonæand during low use days like Monday. This can give you a wholly new look at things.

In the beginning there was mud. The slightest rain turned the rich soil into a mire. Horses, wagons, and men alike sank into its cozy depths, and teams were slowed up to two miles an hour. Frequently the teamster had to unload his wagon and carry its contents to firmer ground, unless a passing driver assisted him by "rolling the wheel." Farmers pushed and pulled, coaxed, exhorted and swore. It was a by-word in the countryside that the most fluent user of profanity got the most of his horses. (circa 1834)

—Marion Knoblauch, *DuPage County Guide*

McDowell Grove Forest Preserve Trail

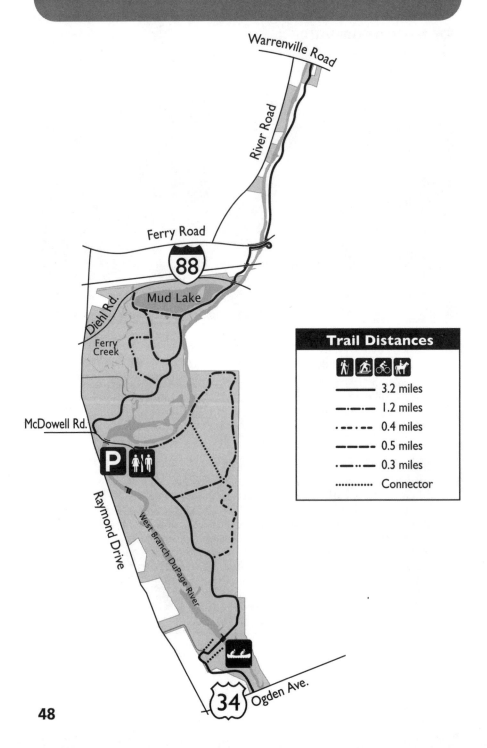

Warrenville Road

River Road

Ferry Road

88

Mud Lake

Diehl Rd.

Ferry Creek

McDowell Rd.

P

Raymond Drive

West Branch DuPage River

34 Ogden Ave.

Trail Distances

———————	3.2 miles
—··—··—	1.2 miles
·——·——	0.4 miles
——— ———	0.5 miles
—·——·——	0.3 miles
·············	Connector

McDowell Grove Forest Preserve Trail

11

NAPERVILLE

TRAIL LENGTH

5 miles

TRAIL SURFACE

Crushed limestone and turf.

LOCATION

McDowell Grove Forest Preserve in Naperville is located on the east side of Raymond Drive south of Interstate 88.

TRAILHEAD LOCATIONS

The entrance and parking area is 0.3 miles south of Diehl Road and approximately one mile north of Ogden Avenue (U.S. Route 34).

TRAIL DESCRIPTION

The McDowell trail connects to the West DuPage River Trail and offers fantastic stretches of a twisting turning route through mature woodlands and open fields along the banks of the West Branch of the DuPage River. The 426-acre McDowell Grove Forest Preserve is a great place to test a rider's or hiker's endurance level. Several looped trail sections make it easy to reduce the mileage of an extensive trek if group members are tiring. Although it doesn't sound very appealing, Mud Lake is a good destination. The distance to scenic Mud Lake is approximately 1.94 miles north from the grove's parking lot.

Two important trail connections have been constructed at McDowell Grove. A 1.8-mile section joins the Cantera trail section north of Diehl Road. This trail segment offers great scenery along the West Branch of the DuPage River to Warrenville Road. Listen for the kingfisher's rachet-sounding call as it dips and glides over the river looking for a fish meal. The path extends into the City of Warrenville's historic area and Warrenville Grove Forest Preserve. From this area it connects to the Illinois Prairie Path and onto Blackwell Forest Preserve's trail system. There is also a five-foot wide limestone screened "carriage path" that parallels Winfield Road north to Cantigny, gardens, war museum, visitor center, mansion and golf course and the Village of Winfield.

The second McDowell Grove section extends 1.5 miles south to Ogden Avenue. This trail section begins at the turnaround at the south end of the McDowell Grove parking lot on the east side of Raymond Drive. It is a typical ten foot-wide limestone trail for approximately 1.25 miles. A quarter mile of asphalt paved trail traverses the previously inaccessible Fawell Dam.

The Fawell Dam is an imposing structure on the landscape. Like most dams, it doesn't have any aesthetic appeal and since it was built in the 1950s it has always looked like an ugly mass of concrete. There has been an attempt by DuPage County dam administrators to soften the appearance and naturalize the setting near the dam through the removal of chain-link fence sections and areas of concrete. Other efforts include planting nine acres of natural seeding and planting more than 140 shrubs and trees. It still looks "dam ugly" and "dam unnatural" but the efforts have helped to soften its appearance.

After the dam crossover the trail follows the western bank of the DuPage River and ends at Ogden Avenue (U.S. Route 34) in Naperville. The City of Naperville will route a trail from this point through the city and connects it with the Naperville Bike Path system and famed Naperville Riverwalk.

TRAVELER'S NOTEBOOK

The trail alignment through the McDowell Grove Forest Preserve is approximately two and a half miles long. A system of trails will travel along the entire length of the West Branch of the DuPage River. The trails through McDowell Grove and the trail's north and south extensions are important links to this regional trail corridor.

For the past fifteen years many infrastructure improvements have been completed at this forest preserve. Additional flood control construction was completed in 2001 at Fawell Dam. The dam and earthen saddle dike protects the downstream areas of Naperville from flooding and backs the water up on forest preserve flood plain.

From 1933 to 1938 the United States government used a portion of McDowell Grove to operate a work camp for President Roosevelt's "Tree Army," the Civilian Conservation Corps. While housed on the property, CCC workers built many solid stone and wood bridges, picnic shelters, scenic dams, boathouses and pathways in area forest preserves. At McDowell Grove in Naperville and Fullersburg Woods in Oak Brook several lagoons were dug by Corps workers. It is estimated that at Camp McDowell up to 3,800 workers were housed in army style barracks during the CCC camp's existence.

During World War II, a secret army training facility and camp housed half of the world's radar equipment under tight security at Camp McDowell. After the attack on Pearl Harbor, the land adjacent to McDowell Grove was purchased by the government. The army needed a secret site to test its radar technology and train men to operate the new technology.

TRAIL TALK

Because of Diehl Road's construction, routing and paving a section of the McDowell Grove Forest Preserve was split off for the benefit of Naperville's automobile transportation corridor. A very controversial decision was made by the DuPage County commissioners that day. Acting as both road builders and conservationists the politicians obviously did not wear their green ecology suits or green hats when they voted. This decision led to a loud citizen outcry for a separate forest preserve board of commissioners. After Illinois state legislation was enacted, an entirely separate forest preserve board was established in December 2002. As a result of the deal for Diehl Road there was a loss of about 11.8 acres of natural area from McDowell Grove Forest Preserve. Was the deal for Diehl Road anything *but* a good deal for nature in this area?

FOR MORE INFORMATION

Visit the Forest Preserve District of DuPage County website at www.dupageforest.com or telephone (630) 933-7200.

DUPAGE COUNTY FOREST PRESERVES

The Forest Preserves are spangles of splendor
Upon the rich raiment of DuPage, the Fair.
Like dewy-eyed daisies limpid and tender
Sewed upon samite priceless and rare!

True men have framed these pictures of glory
And gave them as gifts to the years yet to be
Depicting the charm of Nature's sweet story
Of lake and of river and flower and tree!

They built these fair havens for delicate flowers
And exquisite things surpassing all words.
These glens and thickets and umbrageous bowers
And safe Sanctuaries for beautiful birds!

They fought for the Fair, like chivalry's warriors,
They faced the foe on the forefront of duty.
They stayed the hands of the vandal destroyers
And the feet that trampled and disfigured beauty!

These leafy pavilions in splendor unceasing
Shall grow in charm as years shall sweep by.
A grace and a glory forever increasing
The raptors of soul and spirit and eye!

From *Poems of DuPage County* by Frank Earl Herrick

Meacham Grove Forest Preserve Trail

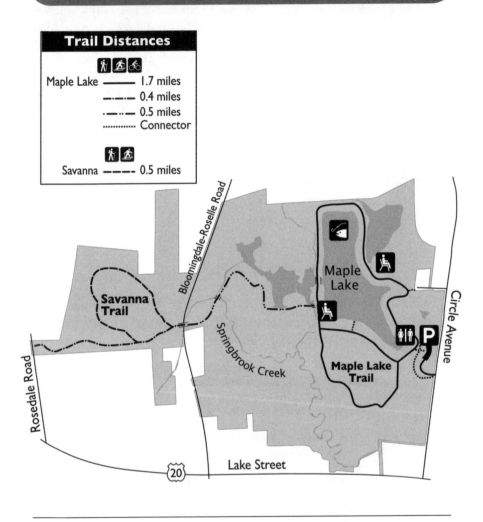

Trail Distances

Maple Lake ————— 1.7 miles
—·—·— 0.4 miles
·—··— 0.5 miles
············ Connector

Savanna ————— 0.5 miles

Maple Lake

Savanna Trail

Bloomingdale-Roselle Road

Springbrook Creek

Maple Lake Trail

Rosedale Road

Circle Avenue

20 Lake Street

Meacham Grove Forest Preserve Trail

11

BLOOMINGDALE

TRAIL LENGTH
2.2 miles

TRAIL SURFACE
Crushed limestone.

LOCATION
Meacham Grove Forest Preserve in Bloomingdale has two parking areas. One entrance is located on Roselle Road approximately one-quarter mile north of Lake Street (U.S. Route 20) and about one mile south of Irving Park Road in Bloomingdale. Another entrance is located on the west side of Circle Avenue, east of Roselle Road and about one quarter mile north of Lake Street.

TRAILHEAD LOCATIONS
If you plan to ride only the trails at Meacham Grove, the Circle Avenue thirty-car parking lot at the east edge of the forest preserve is the best spot to park for an out-and-back destination.

TRAIL DESCRIPTION
The trail loops around the 32-acre Maple Lake area and allows hikers and bikers a couple of different directions to travel for a distance of 1.7 miles.

The looped section to the south offers a nice hill to climb with a bird's eye view of the entire area at the top. The northeastern section of the preserve on the east side of Roselle Road passes by wetlands and provides a nice opportunity to view great egrets, great blue herons and several species of soaring, diving and climbing swallows. The trail also leads path users to the western part of the preserve.

The construction of a bridge over Bloomingdale/Roselle Road established a connection between the eastern and western portions of the preserve. The trail on the west side of the preserve winds its way through forty acres of pristine woods.

Trails that extend through Spring Creek Reservoir and Meacham Grove forest preserves in Bloomingdale is part of the on street and off street North Central Regional Trail system that rolls through the northeastern section of DuPage County and connects to the west with Mallard Lake Forest Preserve. The trail connects to the West Branch Forest Preserve in Bartlett and follows the West Branch of the DuPage River and will eventually incorporate more than twenty miles of continuous forest preserve trails along the river corridor.

TRAVELER'S NOTEBOOK

The 252-acre Meacham Grove Forest Preserve is home to one of the Forest Preserve's District's oldest picnic groves. The Forest Preserve began its acquisition sequence in the 1920s purchasing 40.59 acres of land previously owned by the Meacham family. In its early days it was named Bloomingdale Grove Forest Preserve, but was later changed to honor the original property owners and early settlers.

From the mid-1970s until 2000, there was a variety of developments at Meacham Grove. The abandoned landfill was capped and graded soon after neighbors became actively involved protesting its existence and continued operation.

The quarry was reclaimed by draining, re-grading and enlarging it into the current Maple Lake and multipurpose trail system. In 1996 an embankment along Spring Brook and a spillway dam for the Maple Lake Reservoir were constructed. These structures store floodwaters for the surrounding communities and created a wetland area that supports a variety of native wildlife including beavers, killdeer, egrets, dragonflies and great blue herons.

TRAIL TALK

The west side of Meacham Grove forest preserve is a pristine setting. There is a forty-acre mature forest of maple, oak, walnut and hickory trees that offers great leaf-peeping opportunities during September and October. During April and May prior to full leaf-out, Meacham Grove is known for its thick carpets of wildflowers and is regarded as one of the most beautiful woodlands in DuPage County.

Great displays of the woodland wildflower, the great white trillium, can be seen on the forest floor in early spring and it is said that these were planted during the 1930s by a Bloomingdale women's garden club.

There is a looped footpath about 0.6 miles in length that heads north for hikers and bird watchers. Look above you for the year around avian residents, the downy woodpecker and Cooper's hawk. There are shallow ravines and gentle hilliness in this woodlot. Early in the morning, one can be immersed in the woodland tranquility strolling through this quiet and beautiful spot.

Historical accounts in the *DuPage County Guide* state that Duncklee's Grove part of present day Bloomingdale and Meacham Grove was a "dense grove more than two miles long and one mile or more wide" in 1833.

FOR MORE INFORMATION

Visit the Forest Preserve District of DuPage County website at www.dupageforest.com or telephone (630) 933-7200.

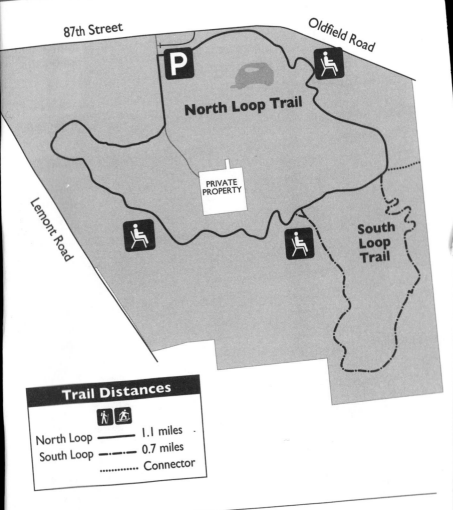

Oldfield Oaks Forest Preserve Trail

87th Street

Oldfield Road

P

North Loop Trail

PRIVATE PROPERTY

Lemont Road

South Loop Trail

Trail Distances

North Loop	——————	1.1 miles
South Loop	—··—··—	0.7 miles
	············	Connector

Morton Arboretum Biking and Hiking

LISLE

TRAIL LENGTH

4.8 miles for bicycling (arboretum members only) and 14 miles of hiking trails.

TRAIL SURFACE

The narrow asphalt roadway is open for bicycling on the east side of the Morton Arboretum. Bikes are not allowed off the road or on any other trails.

Meadow Lake has a paved 0.6-mile hiking trail that is flat and accessible for people that are mobility challenged. Another paved hiking or strolling path extends for one mile from the Visitor Center to the arboretum's west side and across the West Branch of the DuPage River bridge to the Thornhill building. It is somewhat of a steep climb up to the Thornhill building.

There are more than twelve miles of wood-chipped, turf and dirt pathways throughout the 1,700-acre Morton Arboretum. Trails are looped and out and back routes that wind their way thru extensive plant collections and landscape exhibits.

DIRECTIONS

Located at 4100 Illinois Route 53 the main entrance is at Park Avenue on the east side of Illinois Route 53 in Lisle. The entrance is one-half mile north of the Interstate 88 tollway on the east side of Illinois Route 53 and south of Butterfield Road (Illinois Route 56).

TRAILHEAD LOCATIONS

Morton Arboretum members who want to bicycle on the east side road system must park their cars at the main parking lot on the east side.

Hikers can take their pick of parking areas located along the road system.

Trail Description

Visitors can hike the more than fourteen miles of trail or ride the 4.8-mile east side road system at the 1,700-acre arboretum. There are more than 3,400 plant species from fifty-nine different countries to view, smell, touch and learn about. The road system used for biking is a closed loop through the east side's oak, pine, elm, and maple collections. Beside the fresh smells of pine trees bike riders will see a beautiful marsh, Crabapple Lake, Meadow Lake and many northern Illinois native plants and animals. The bicycling road system is asphalt paved and it has a gently rolling topography suitable for a most family friendly excursion.

Portions of the hiking trails are paved and easily accessed by people of all abilities. Other sections are narrow turf or wood-chipped trails that meander and curl through the woods and prairie. The beautiful woodlands, prairie, wetlands, small lakes, the East Branch of the DuPage River and glorious gardens feature globally rare and native plant materials. Many seasonal explorations are highlighted by the arboretum's staff member tours, special weekend events and Web site descriptions.

Traveler's Notebook

Visitors must pay an admission fee or join as a member. The relaxing bike rides are open to Morton Arboretum members only on Friday and Saturday evenings from 5 p.m. to 9 p.m., May through August. The roadway is narrow and helmets are strongly recommended. The offering is intended for families and those who want to take a cruising ride and coast to observe the beauty of nature and plant collections along the way. Helmets are strongly recommended if not required.

The grounds are open every day of the year from 7 a.m. until 5 p.m. during Central Standard Time and from 7 a.m. until 7 p.m. during daylight savings time. The arboretum prohibits alcohol, pets, grilling, active sports and bicycles (except for members at designated times). The Morton Arboretum provides a safe secure atmosphere for visitors.

Trail Talk

With more than 3,400 types of trees, shrubs and other plants here you can have a bloomin' good time in the spring or a spectacular fall color exploration. All seasons can be enjoyed and the museum staff members make it fun and easy to learn about the collections and get involved in a program, self-guided or guided tour. There are many special events and instructional programs offered to homeowners, families, children, landscape professionals and gardeners throughout the year.

Volunteers assist with all phases of the operation and they are an appreciated human resource that is an essential component that helps to make the Morton Arboretum one of the best outdoor museums on the planet. It is an interesting and enjoyable place to visit with always something different going on or several new varieties of plants to look at and learn about. The Arboretum is a good place to support by joining as a member and then you can ride and hike to your heart's content.

Once you join you can also dine in the Ginkgo Café, visit the Sterling Morton Library or ask the experts questions about ailing plants at the Plant Clinic. One of the most striking landscapes a visitor can witness is Daffodil Glade when it is in full bloom. Other highlights include the Schulenberg

Prairie restoration project, the flowering crabapple tr of the small lakes offering nature's reflections.

Joy Morton was the founder of Morton Salt Compa founder of Arbor Day. The Morton Arboretum was e promote conservation and study of trees and plants. shrub collections from fifty-nine countries. Mae Watts first proposed the idea of setting aside the Chicago, Railroad property as a path way (which became the Il worked here for many years.

FOR MORE INFORMATION

Visit the website at www.mortonarb.org or telephone (63

Photo courtesy of Morton Arboretum.

Oldfield Oaks Forest Preserve Trail

13

DARIEN

TRAIL LENGTH

A two-mile, six-foot wide looped trail for hiking and strolling. Bicycling and horseback riding are not permitted.

TRAIL SURFACE

Crushed limestone.

LOCATION

The Oldfield Oaks Forest Preserve is in Darien. It is located on the south side of Oldfield Road, on the east side of Lemont Road, south of Eighty-seventh Street.

TRAILHEAD LOCATIONS

A twenty-car parking lot is located on the south side of Oldfield Road east of Lemont Road in Darien.

TRAIL DESCRIPTION

There are two narrow looped trails to hike. The trail loops are flat and they curl around and through ecologically diverse and globally rare oak wood-lands. The narrow walking trail provides an up close view of nature for people of all ages and a wide range of ambling ability. It is a very family-friendly hiking trail that was designed to protect rare and beautiful natural elements and reduce the number of bicyclists that are attracted to longer, wider trails.

TRAVELER'S NOTEBOOK

This seventy-eight acre parkland may not be the largest forest preserve but it is a diverse natural area that features small prairie remnants, rare oak woodlands and wondrous wetlands. Because of this preserve's size and rare ecosystems, a narrower trail for hiking and strolling was developed to lessen habitat fragmentation and to protect the native plants and animals that live there.

During a hike around the trail in the spring, visitors may catch whiffs of wild Burdick's leek, wild onion and invasive garlic mustard in the cool moist air. From the trail observant hikers can spot the spectacular Jack-in-the-Pulpit in bloom, lavender colored wild geranium, the white flowered bloodroot, the green umbrella plant or May apple and various sedges.

As summer's long days arrive, ox-eye daisies, prairie dock, sawtooth and pale-leaved sunflowers, black-eyed Susan make plenty of eye-candy to view. During the summer the unique scent of wild bergamot and ripened succulent fruits of colorful wild gooseberry, black raspberry, common blackberry, elderberry and riverbank grape offer a food source to song-birds. Listening and watching at the berry bush locations is a good place for trailside bird watching.

In the late summer and fall old-field and early goldenrod and heath, side-flowering, hairy, Drummond's, panicled and New England asters add a color palette and to Oldfield Oaks landscape. And of course a variety of tree canopies add both intense yellow and orange leaf color. Dusty maroon and brown colors seep into the treetops as fall season wanes. From bottom to top in a single cottonwood tree the green leaves soften into sunlit yellows and explode into shimmering gold. Red-leafed vines of the Virginia creeper and poison ivy climb white, scarlet, burr, black and white oak tree trunks.

TRAIL TALK

Oldfield Oaks Forest Preserve is one of the most recent acquisitions of the Forest Preserve District of DuPage County. Many of the neighbors in the area recognized the irreplaceable beauty of this tranquil setting and voiced their support for its preservation. This seventy-eight acre forest preserve was acquired by the Forest Preserve District of DuPage County in 1998.

FOR MORE INFORMATION

Visit the Forest Preserve District of DuPage County website at www.dupageforest.com or telephone (630) 933-7200.

EARLY PIONEER QUOTE ABOUT THE ILLINOIS FRONTIER

A few steps more, and a beautiful prairie suddenly opened to our view. At first we only received the impressions of its general beauty. With longer gaze, all its distinctive features were revealed, lying in profound response under the warm light of an afternoon's summer sun. In its dented and irregular outline of wood, its varied surface interspersed with clumps of oaks of centuries growth, its tall grass, with seed stalks from six to ten feet high, like tall and slender reed waving on a gentle breeze, the whole presenting a magnificence of park scenery, complete from the hand of Nature, and unrivaled by the same sort of scenery in European art. For once the reality came up to the picture of imagination.

—Morris Birdbeck, 1816

ITCHING TO TELL TREKKERS ABOUT POISON IVY

Poison ivy is a hardy plant that lives in many places. It grows in most DuPage County forest preserves and alongside many trail locations. Since it grows in areas that have been disturbed, trailsides are excellent places for the ivy to take up residence! It is a real good idea for outdoor adventurers to know what it looks like.

Although it has three mitten-shaped leaves, from two to four inches in length, poison ivy can be tough to identify. The middle leaf usually protrudes on a longer stalk from the single leaves on each side. The leaves alternate from the main stem. Berries along the stem are green in summer and change to a whitish color in winter. In autumn the leaves turn a beautiful crimson color. Be careful picking up colorful leaves in autumn! Like any terrifying alien invader poison ivy has a changing physical appearanceælook, it's a plant! No, it's a vine! Now it's a bush! It's *Super Plant!*

The uroshiol oil of the plant produces the irritant that causes a skin rash. The oil is present in all the plant parts at all times of the year and can remain in a dead plant for a long time. Even smoke from a burning poison ivy plant contains the oil and can cause problems and serious irritation. Have you ever tried to scratch or itch your lungs? It isn't possible.

If you think you have come into contact with poison ivy you may need to seek medical attention to lessen the severity of the rash.

On a positive note, poison ivy encourages rambling outdoorsman to stay on the trail and it provides a food source for many animals through the winter.

James "Pate" Philip State Park Trail

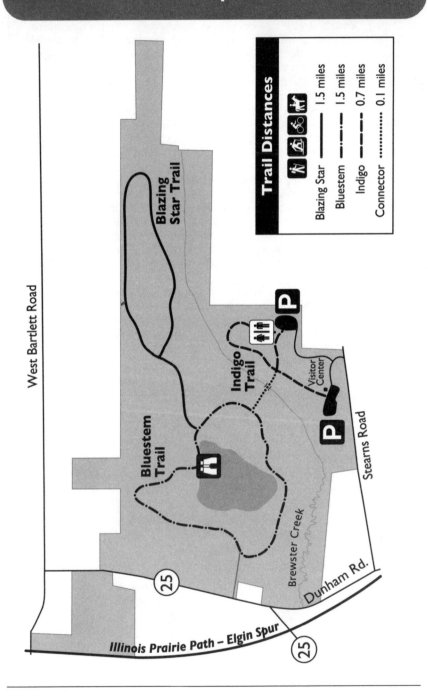

James "Pate" Philip State Park Trail

BARTLETT

This trail was formerly known as Tri-County State Park.

TRAIL LENGTH

3.77 miles of looped trails extending through restored prairies and wetlands.

TRAIL SURFACE

Crushed limestone.

LOCATION

James "Pate" Philip State Park (formerly Tri-County State Park) located in Bartlett is located on the north side of Stearns Road just west of Powis Road. The address is 2054 S. Stearns Road in Bartlett.

TRAILHEAD LOCATIONS

The parking lot located on the north side of Stearns Road is the only location to access the trail system.

TRAIL DESCRIPTION

Nearly four miles of multipurpose trails wind through James "Pate" Philip State Park's 501 acres.

The Bluestem Trail circles a marsh and intersects the location where DuPage, Kane and Cook counties meet. There is a short segment that leads to an overlook of a marsh. The Blazing Star Trail extends to the park's outer reaches and further into the restored tallgrass prairie.

Both trails cross over flat to gently rolling terrain and as a result are good for touring youngsters or beginners just learning how to ride.

TRAVELER'S NOTEBOOK

This recently constructed state park had its beginning in 1989 when the Illinois General Assembly appropriated $10 million to the Illinois Department of Natural Resources for this state park's acquisition. There aren't many other state parks in northern Illinois so it is fitting that the purchase of the 501 acres would cover ground in three counties.

In 1991, the Illinois Department of Natural Resources developed a restoration plan to guide preliminary restoration activities at the site. Since most of the property had previously been used for agricultural purposes the park is a work in progress. The flora and fauna is sure to flourish as natural resource professionals remove hedgerows and conduct prescribed burns to remnant native plant communities at the site.

The James "Pate" Philip Visitor Center opened in the summer of 2003. It contains many exciting exhibits that tell the land's story through photomurals and through interactive displays that show prairie highlights and the need to protect and rebuild this valuable ecosystem. There is also a small theater that features a video that recounts the land changes that have occurred in the area from the glaciers that sculpted it to the settlers, farmers and developers who tamed it to the individuals who are now attempting to restore its native wildlife. For more information call the James "Pate" Philip State Park at (847) 429-4670.

TRAIL TALK

The wetland is one of northern Illinois rarest ecosystems. Only three percent of DuPage County remains wetland. Researchers estimate that DuPage County was once covered by 60 percent of wet and seepy ground.

During the late 1970s, restoration ecologists began to restore DuPage County's marshy land. It was recognized by many area ecologists and land managers that the prairie character that made Illinois the "prairie state" was being diminished. Restoration along the forks of Brewster Creek in Pratt's Wayne Woods Forest Preserve began in the late 1990s. Miles of clay tiles that were originally installed during the late 1800s and early 1900s to drain agricultural fields were exposed and broken. As soils became saturated again, wet prairies and marshes developed. These actions help to create habitat for many species of plants and animals to survive and flourish.

James "Pate" Philip State Park area is fast becoming a wildlife magnet, especially since 3,432-acre Pratt's Wayne Woods is contiguous to the east and south of the park.

Together James "Pate" Philip State Park and Pratt's Wayne Woods Forest Preserve improve the integrity of the ecosystems complex and ability to function as nature intended. Long and wide wildlife corridors are established allowing all life to roam (and loaf) a little better without so many human impacts. There is also the opportunity to invite back more plant and animal species into the life zone.

Already breeding populations of sandhill cranes, Blanding's turtles, yellow-headed blackbirds and Henslow's sparrows are breeding and raising young in some of the restored wetlands and grasslands. There will be more to come back to this large expanse of nature.

Restorations of remnant ecosystems are common and well-supported in northern Illinois. The rapid rate of agricultural and urban development destroyed much the natural communities which existed in DuPage County.

Prairies, oak savannas, woodlands, marshes, fens and meadows once so common in Illinois have all but disappeared. What remains are small islands or clusters of natural areas that require protection and active management. Restoration strategies include prescribed burns, deer culling, selective cutting, some herbiciding, overseeding and the reintroduction of certain plant and animal species. Restoration management activities can alter the deteriorating effects taking place within these biologically rich remnant ecosystems.

PREPARATIONS FOR BICYCLISTS

- Buy a bike that fits your body. When your foot is flat on the pedal and your leg is extended there should be a slight bend at the knee, and not completely straightened out.

- Be sure your seat (on the bicycle) is properly adjusted and tightened.

- Check the brakes to be sure they operate properly.

- Wear a helmet that fits properly.

- Rearview mirrors provide added visibility.

- Wear UV protective sunglasses to reduce damaging sun glare and to protect the eyes from small rocks.

- Protect your skin by using sunscreen even on cloudy days.

- Know how to make simple repairs like changing a flat tire.

- Carry a spare tube or two.

- Use headlights and tail lights if you are riding early in the morning or at dusk.

- Know the route, obey all traffic signs, railroad crossings and remember that "wheels yield to heels".

- Use hand signals to indicate your intention to turn.

- Wear brightly colored clothes for high visibility.

Springbrook Prairie Forest Preserve Trail

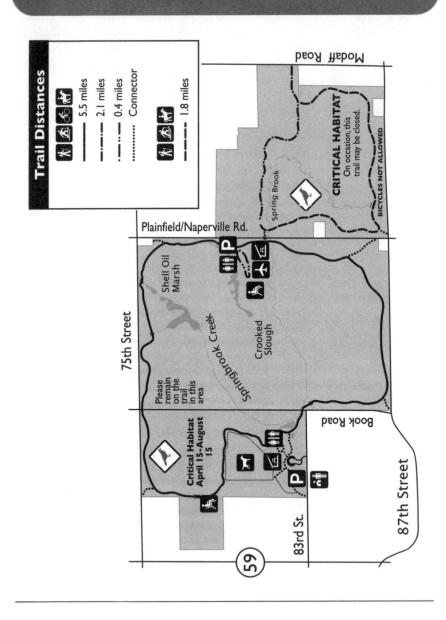

Trail Distances

— 5.5 miles
—·— 2.1 miles
—··— 0.4 miles
········ Connector

—— 1.8 miles

Modaff Road

Plainfield/Naperville Rd.

Spring Brook

CRITICAL HABITAT
On occasion, this
trail may be closed.

BICYCLES NOT ALLOWED

Shell Oil
Marsh

Springbrook Creek

75th Street

Crooked
Slough

Please
remain
on the
trail
in this
area

**Critical Habitat
April 15–August
15**

Book Road

83rd St.

87th Street

59

Springbrook Prairie Forest Preserve Trail

NAPERVILLE

TRAIL LENGTH

Springbrook has a 9.5-mile loop trail.

TRAIL SURFACE

Crushed limestone, mowed turf and a short 0.3-mile asphalt trail.

LOCATION

Springbrook Prairie is located in Naperville on both east and west side of Plainfield-Naperville Road, one-half mile south of 75th Street. This forest preserve extends south to 83rd Street and beyond. There are two parking lots that offer trailside access.

TRAILHEAD LOCATIONS

Access points to the trail are located on the west side of Plainfield-Naperville Road. Further to the south and west a larger, 100-car parking lot is open on the north side of 83rd Street.

TRAIL DESCRIPTION

At the 1,849-acre Springbrook Prairie Forest Preserve in Naperville bikers and hikers will find that many amenities and mighty fine facilities await them. The trailside area near 83rd Street offers a large parking lot, water, flush toilets and a picnic area with a shelter placed within a surrounding savanna. There is also a large pooch park for visiting canine pals to romp and roam leash free.

More than eight miles of trails have been added in loop fashion and provide touring trekkers views of a unique grassland ecosystem. Wide open views of swaying grasses and opportunities to observe rare ground nesting bird species are here to enjoy. Birding is excellent and a keen eye might see one of several native bird species including; bob-o-links, meadowlarks or red-tailed hawks. A keener set of eyes might recognize the endangered yellow-headed blackbird, Henslow's sparrow or northern harrier.

On June 5, 2004, National Trails Day, Secretary of the Interior Gale Norton designated Springbrook Prairie and Herrick Lake trails as National Recreation Trails. This national recreational trail designation recognizes that both routes are exemplary trails of local and regional significance and are recognized as part of America's national system of trails.

The Springbrook Prairie Trail loops around the prairie's outskirts so that wild things can take refuge in the preserve's interior and habitat doesn't get fragmented. It isn't unusual to spot a coyote loping through the interior in search of mice or voles at dawn or dusk. During a spring hunting foray, a coyote that favors a meal of Canada goose eggs, may be willing to risk the wrath of aggressively protective Canada geese. When approached by a stalking coyote, the geese may defend or vacate the nest and clutch of eggs.

Because this is a prairie trail, users will not be able to locate much shade. It is a good idea to put on a hat, sunglasses and sun screen and bring lots of water before venturing out on these trails. A strong headwind will offer stiff resistance to cyclists. Keep in mind that this is a looped trail and the wind will eventually be at your back pushing you along.

The trail is mostly flat with a few short hills popping up and over the countryside. Springbrook Prairie Trail is a successful blend of ecological protection and recreational opportunity that adds up to great wildlife watching. Visitors will enjoy crossing three bridges and the possibility of observing amphibians and unique avian wetland waders in their marsh homes close to boardwalks.

If you're not riding or hiking and have a dog, there is a thirty-six acre, off-leash dog area that is great fun for Bowser and canine lovers. When lots of dogs are running around they can be entertaining to watch. For many mutt strutters, this doggy play lot offers as much a social occasion for the owners as it is does for their dogs.

TRAVELER'S NOTEBOOK

During the 1970s this area was named Dragon Lake Forest Preserve. The original master plan to build a 200-acre dragon shaped lake included a beach and campground. These intense recreational development plans were scaled back once people began to better understand the area's special ecological significance.

In 1994, the name of the preserve was officially changed to Springbrook Prairie. An advisory committee was formed to create a second master plan for this preserve. The group consisted of neighbors, special interest groups and staff members from Naperville Park District, the city of Naperville, and the Forest Preserve District of DuPage County. It was Aldo Leopold who said in so many words that, "the secret to conservation and protecting nature is to control man's innate desire to build something."

The key elements of the plan called for the protection of three Illinois state-endangered species: the northern harrier, the short-eared owl and the Henslow's sparrow. The large expanses of natural areas to explore include savanna, prairies, wetlands and streams. Crews of dedicated volunteers have worked hard to restore Springbrook Prairie grassland habitat to its strongest biological diversity.

Fence lines have been removed connecting and extending grassland habitat and wetlands have been successfully created. The removal of box elder, mulberry, black cherry, Osage orange, honey locust and elm trees improve nesting and feeding areas. Nesting grassland bird species at Springbrook Prairie include; sedge wrens, bob-o-links, eastern meadowlarks, dickcissels and grassland and savannah sparrows.

Spring Brook, a tributary of the DuPage River, has been selected for a waterway restoration effort. The innovative project will involve the reconfiguration of one and a half miles of the stream course, re-creating natural meanders and reconnecting the stream with its historic flood plain. The stream suffers from erosion but it also has excellent water quality and is rated by ecologists as the most biologically diverse stream in DuPage County. It is home to many mussel and fish species. The stream's condition can only be improved through these novel restoration efforts.

TRAIL TALK

Springbrook Prairie Forest Preserve is the third largest forest preserve in DuPage County. A rare bird that nests at Springbrook Prairie is the clay-colored sparrow. The sparrow nests on the edges of grassy woodlands. It has the unusual habit of lining its nest with any hair that is available and has been known to pull hair out of a sleeping dog. So much said for "letting a sleeping dog lie." In May black-capped chickadees will also gather hair or fur to line a layer of their nest. Nature lovers can substitute fur for fat in suet feeders this time of year.

The red fox is a resident to Springbrook Prairie and by their nature, foxes are predators to ground-nesting birds. There are many interesting details about the red fox. One is that the male in springtime is a desperate suitor. Nature dictates that female foxes, called vixen, are biologically prepared for mating during a maximum of six days each year. The male red fox uses scent markings to define his territory, providing an olfactory "occupancy notice" to other nonresident males. Then he begins calling and listening for a vixen's response. The howls, yips and piercing shrieks can be easily heard usually breaking the quiet night. The fox's voice can carry over the fields for long distances. These night sounds begin and randomly increase and decrease in volume until the would-be couple meets. Once pair bonding takes place, the couple digs a new den or remodels an existing groundhog den in order to prepare to raise a litter of kits.

During the 1980s there was a story floating around and told by Springbrook Prairie neighbors and some forest preserve personnel that an elk was grazing around the vast grassland. Forest Preserve District sources received many reports from individuals who described a close encounter with an elk.

Some first-hand reports were seemingly reliable observations but others were a bit of a stretch. The sightings occurred in the years before facilities were constructed at Springbrook Prairie and prior to the construction of housing developments that surround the area today. No one ever did confirm the elk's presence and the reports of an elk eventually ceased.

What is interesting is that the elk has been extirpated for so long from Illinois that there is no mention of the ungulate in the Illinois Game Code that sets regulations for hunting and fishing. Since the animal does not officially exist there is nothing that protects elk, no hunting season for the critters or no ban on hunting the animals either. Do these facts open the door to the possibility that the hooved and meat stacked beast could have been killed and carted off without there being a sport hunting violation?

FOR MORE INFORMATION

Visit the Forest Preserve District of DuPage County website at www.dupageforest.com or telephone (630) 933-7200.

Photo courtesy of Dick Todd.

KEEPING DUPAGE COUNTY'S TRAILS SAFE

Keeping trails safe and being safe on the trails is everyone's priority. Trail users can help keep trails safe and well maintained by being watchful during an excursion.

In DuPage County new signs have been placed at strategic locations and provide trail trekkers with phone numbers to call in case of an emergency. There are different numbers to call to report maintenance and safety problems depending on where you are located. Of course anytime there is an emergency of a serious nature, calling 911 is the most immediate way to get help or report a criminal activity.

In the event of emergencies and after-hours issues along the Great Western Trail and the Illinois Prairie Path call the DuPage County Sheriff's Office at (630) 407-2100. To report trail maintenance issues along the Great Western Trail and Illinois Prairie Path the DuPage County Department of Transportation should be notified at (630) 407-6900.

The Forest Preserve District of DuPage County Office of Law Enforcement can be reached by calling (630) 933-7240 and the DuPage County Sheriff's Department patrol DuPage County's trail systems.

Overhanging limbs, fallen trees and suspicious activity on DuPage County Forest Preserve District grounds can all be reported by calling (630) 933-7200. The line can be reached 24-hours a day, seven days a week.

Law enforcement agencies encourage participation of trail users to become additional eyes and ears watching for problems on the trails. Paths are made safer when everyone participates in a community policing effort. If anything unusual is spotted citizens are encouraged to carry and use their cell phones to report situations. It is not a good idea to become confrontational or to try to solve a problem alone.

Trained volunteers in uniforms also routinely patrol the forest preserve trails. Volunteer trail patrollers attend training classes to learn trail routes, basic first-aid and emergency response procedures. The helpful and friendly volunteers carry maps and information about DuPage County's labyrinths of trails, paths and on and off road bike routes. They are usually individuals who ride lots of miles so their voice of first hand experiences has never been known to steer an inquisitive, lost or confused trekker in the wrong direction. They routinely cover miles of trails. If you are interested in becoming a volunteer trail patrol member with the Forest Preserve District of DuPage County call (630) 933-7681.

Spring Creek Reservoir Forest Preserve Trail

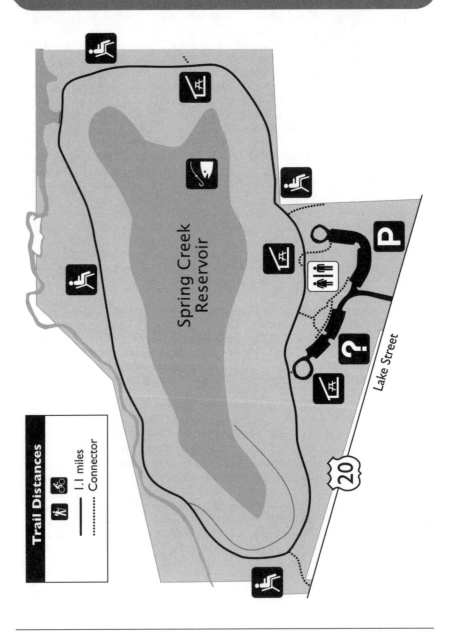

Spring Creek Reservoir

Lake Street

20

Trail Distances

— 1.1 miles
········ Connector

Spring Creek Reservoir Forest Preserve Trail

16

BLOOMINGDALE

TRAIL LENGTH
1.1 mile

TRAIL SURFACE
Asphalt.

LOCATION
Spring Creek Reservoir in Bloomingdale entrance is located on Lake Street (U.S. Route 20), one-quarter mile east of Glen Ellyn Road and one-quarter mile west of Medinah Road.

TRAILHEAD LOCATIONS
The parking lot located on the north side of Lake Street (U.S. Route 20) is the most accessible location.

TRAIL DESCRIPTION
At only seventy-five acres, Spring Creek Reservoir would be an easy place to pedal past. This trail and its pleasant surroundings should not be ignored. It is very flat, asphalt surfaced, and more than a mile long. Because there are no roads to cross, it is nearly perfect for mobility impaired people, beginner bicyclists or those who want to learn to in-line skate. This extremely popular trail circles the approximate forty-acre Spring Lake, a reservoir that was built as a huge catch basin in order to reduce the potential for flooding of private properties near Spring Creek within the Salt Creek watershed.

The trail is resurfaced and maintained on a regular schedule. Other improvements include the addition of 0.8 miles of trail in two sections that connect with the Village of Bloomingdale's trail system. The area includes a fifty-person reservable picnic shelter, flush restroom facility and additional parking. Trails that extend through Spring Creek Reservoir and Meacham Grove forest preserves in Bloomingdale are part of the North Central DuPage County Regional Trail system and roll through the northeastern section of DuPage County and connect to the west with Mallard Lake Forest Preserve and to the West Branch Regional Trail.

TRAVELER'S NOTEBOOK

Looking over the silvery blue water and the large concrete spillway structure it is hard to believe that the area was once devoted acres of agricultural use covered with fields of corn, hay, soybeans and wheat. At one time the open land in this now highly developed area spread as far as the eye could see. Later it was mined as a gravel pit. The site was a barren quarry until 1987 when the Forest Preserve District of DuPage County acquired it and reclaimed it as a recreational area and reservoir that stores floodwater for Spring Creek. The average depth of the reservoir's water is fifteen feet but after heavy rains, it can fluctuate to a depth of fifty-five feet.

Call (630) 933-7248 for more information.

TRAIL TALK

There are three benches made of recycled plastic bottles situated along the asphalt trail. If you feel more like relaxing than hiking or biking, the reservoir's sparkling waters can be viewed from any of them. On a sunny warm summer's day it is a great spot to watch a flowing, rolling variety of strollers, rollers and joggers. In-line skaters find this area a great location to roll around without the worry of automobile traffic.

After a good amount of rain, the floodwaters from Spring Creek cascade over the intake structure and fill the reservoir. Additional parking and a short trail segment have been constructed on property now owned by the forest preserve. Old-timers might recall that this location was once the site of the amusement park named "Adventureland." This is still a good place for an adventure!

FOR MORE INFORMATION

Visit the Forest Preserve District of DuPage County website at www.dupageforest.com or telephone (630) 933-7200.

A RIDE DURING LATE AUGUST.

The orb weaver spiders and all their trappings are in great supply this time of year. If you happen to be the first riders out on the trail it means you break the silver strands of the spiders webs strung across the trail. I don't feel anything crawling around on my neck. It's easy to imagine lines of lacey strands gathering across my body as distance is covered. I think of Gulliver's Travels and wonder whether all the lacey strands I am collecting could ever bind me and slow me to a standstill.

DuPage County has benefited from a proud tradition of civic involvement in her trails. Concerned citizens led the organization of America's very first rail-to-trail conversion, the famous Illinois Prairie Path.

Letter to the Editor
Chicago Tribune
September 1963

Dear Editor:

We are human beings. We are able to walk upright on two feet. We need a footpath. Right now there is a chance for Chicago and its suburbs to have a footpath, a long one.

The right of way of the Aurora electric road lies waiting. If we have courage and foresight, such as made possible the Long trail in Vermont and the Appalachian trail from Maine to Georgia, and the network of the public footpaths in Britain, then we can create from this strip a proud resource.

Look ahead some years into the future. Imagine yourself going for a walk on an autumn day. Choose some part of the famed Illinois footpath. Where the highway crosses it, you enter over a stile. . . The grass is cut and garden flowers bloom in great beds. This part you may learn is maintained by the Chicago Horticultural Society. Beyond the garden you enter a forest again, maintained by the Morton Arboretum. At its edge begins a long stretch of water with mud banks, maintained for water birds and waders, by the Ornithological society. You notice an abundance of red-fruited shrubs. The birds have the Audubon societies to thank for those. You rest on one of the stout benches provided by the Prairie club, beside a thicket of wild crab trees planted by the Garden Club of Illinois.

Then you walk thru prairie again. Four Boy Scouts pass. They are hiking the entire length of the trail. This fulfills a requirement for some merit badge. A troop of Scouts is planting acorns in a grove of cottonwood trees. Most of the time you find yourself in prairie or woodland of native Illinois plants. These stretches of trail need little or no upkeep. You come to one stretch, a long stretch, where nothing has been done. But university students are identifying and listing plants. The University of Chicago ecology department is in charge of this strip. They are watching to see what time and nature will do. . .

That is all in the future, the possible future. Right now the right of way lies waiting, and many hands are itching for it. Many bulldozers are drooling.

May Watts

Waterfall Glen Forest Preserve Trail

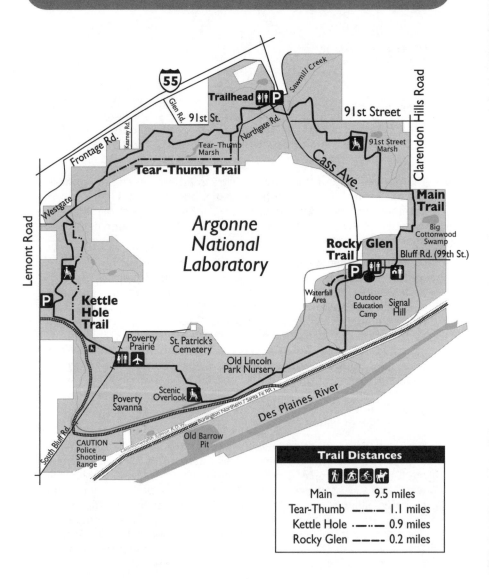

Waterfall Glen
Forest Preserve Trail

17

DARIEN

TRAIL LENGTH

9.5 miles of looped trail.

TRAIL SURFACE

9.5 miles of crushed limestone. The Waterfall Glen trail is groomed for diagonal and skate style cross-country skiing when there is adequate snow cover.

LOCATION

There is an entrance to this expansive forest preserve on the north side of Northgate Road, just west of Cass Avenue. From Interstate 55, exit Cass south to Northgate Road. Look for an Argonne Laboratory entrance sign and turn right on Northgate Road. The parking lot will be immediately on the right or south side of the road. The Outdoor Education Camp parking lot can be accessed from the south side of Bluff Road (99th Street), which intersects with Cass Avenue.

There is a second newer parking lot at an existing three-way intersection opposite 101st Street and on the east side of Lemont Road. This lot provides access to the western trail section and access to the Southern DuPage Regional Trail.

TRAILHEAD LOCATIONS

Three parking areas offer access to the Waterfall Glen trail system. The Outdoor Education Camp and the Northgate Road parking lots have two latrines and a hand pump for water. The Northgate Road parking lot offers more parking spaces including pull through spaces for horse trailers. This lot is popular and often fills to capacity faster than the parking area at the outdoor education camp. On beautiful summer and fall days when both lots fill to capacity it is not uncommon for people to park their cars on the shoulders of Northgate or Bluff Road and 91st Street.

The newer trailhead and entrance drive is located on the east side of Lemont Road (County Highway 9) is a high-volume arterial roadway and it offers access at safe intersection with traffic signals and a left-hand turn lane for southbound vehicles for southbound vehicles entering the preserve from Lemont Road. At the northeastern edge of the parking area there is a point of access within 300 feet into the main trail and western part of

Waterfall Glen. The trail also ties into the countywide Southern DuPage Regional Trail System constructed on the north side of 101st Street, between Woodward Avenue and Lemont Road. This newer parking lot will not accommodate horse trailers.

TRAIL DESCRIPTION

The Waterfall Glen looped trail is simply the best trail network there is in DuPage County. It has hills, gurgling brooks, overlooks at the top of steep hills, historical remnants, beautiful scenery consisting of several different ecosystems. Planted pine groves smell crisp and wonderful, oak-maple woodlands provide colorful beauty especially in autumn and spring, savannas and prairies are rich with flowers and spiraling butterflies and the marshes with beaver and muskrat lodges provide a backdrop for bikers and hikers wanting peak outdoor experiences. Providing a setting of quiet solitude, this forest preserve is the closest you'll come to a wilderness experience in DuPage County.

Expert horseback riders, bicyclists, hikers, runners and cross-country skiers congregate at Waterfall Glen. With so many recreational users, the trails can become busy. A speeding bicyclist, galloping horseback rider or pack of runners can be traveling hell-bent for election while zipping around any bend in the trail. It is best to keep your eyes open and stay on the inside portion of the trail. Ride single file and remember some people are crazy.

The extensive loop trail circles through the 2,374-acre forest preserve around Argonne Laboratory. Be sure to carry a map! It is easy to get lost at Waterfall Glen. If it isn't too cold and if you haven't run out of water, being lost can be invigorating and challenging. It is important to try to enjoy all your outdoor recreational experiences even if you feel hopelessly lost.

Orienteering clubs in the area also use an orienteering course that is set up for novice through expert level participants. Orienteering is a challenging outdoor activity that involves finding your way through the woods and around the water with a compass, topography map and measured paces. Several routes are laid out and open for use year-round. Groups can check out maps, compasses and related nature activity sheets by calling Fullersburg Woods Environmental Education Center at (630) 850-8110.

Orienteering aficionados are a breed of their own. They are hard-core and like to challenge themselves by going through and across the roughest terrain. Like any sport, orienteering has its own nomenclature. For example, a "crawl" is a section that is difficult to get through without crouching, running or chasing through a buckthorn forest like a black bear. This group believes in rip-stop clothing material and wears competitive equipment that by design will not get snagged or caught on low hanging branches or other rough stuff.

TRAVELER'S NOTEBOOK

Waterfall Glen Forest Preserve contains more wildlife and plant varieties than any other forest preserve in DuPage County. Records taken by wildlife managers indicate there are more than 240 different species of animals. These include seventeen fish species, eleven amphibians, nineteen reptiles, thirty mammals and more than 160 bird species. Birds such as the oven bird, prothonotary warbler, scarlet tanager, red-headed woodpecker and indigo bunting are residents at Waterfall Glen. The federally endangered Hines emerald dragonfly makes its home in the wet seeps of fens at this preserve.

This biologically diverse area has had more than 600 native plant species recorded by plant ecologists. How many can you come to know? The area includes seventy-five percent of all plants known to grow naturally in DuPage County. Visitors should occasionally get off their bike and explore areas adjacent to the trails to witness the glorious scents, sights and sounds of prairies, savannas, oak-maple woodlands and planted pine groves at Waterfall Glen. With so much life preserved at this area it is important that users also remain responsible, tread lightly and be careful in these sensitive areas not to damage these globally rare, one of kind areas. In this way Waterfall Glen will remain intact for the younger generations of trail enthusiasts.

The topography of Waterfall Glen has been shaped by the Wisconsin Glacial Episode. Steep hills are a rare commodity in DuPage County but not at Waterfall Glen. The ridges, stream channels and potholes scattered through Waterfall Glen are a result of glaciers. The Des Plaines River valley was cut by glacial melt waters and from a postglacial lake that covered most of the Chicago land area.

Many streams cut through the glacial deposits down to the Des Plaines River bed. There are steep ridges and limestone outcroppings to dazzle hikers and provide ramped down fun for bicyclists.

DuPage County's only artesian well pushes up through the rock near one of the manmade quarries. The rising icy cold water is caused by pressure on the groundwater from the higher land overlooking the well. It can be fun to explore the remote southwestern portion of the preserve and locate this unusual feature. Trail users are on their own when drinking from the artesian well because the health department does not condone its use as a drinking fountain.

TRAIL TALK

Waterfall Glen Trivia

In the mid-1600s Pere Marquette and Louis Joliet were the first to blaze trails in the area. They mostly paddled the water trail provided by the Des Plaines River.

There is a vantage point named Signal Hill overlooking the Des Plaines River valley. Historical accounts indicate that this was where Indians camped and signaled fur traders and Native Americans up and downstream. Smoke signals, an amazing communication method, could take place over great distances. Damp grass under a pyramid of brush would create different arrangements of dense columns of smoke. When covered and removed with a hide or blanket the smoldering fire would produce spirals of smoke in different-sized patterns released at differently timed intervals.

The telegraphing clouds could also be created in somewhat different colors by burning different natural materials. Signal fire announcements were also used at night by igniting blazing rows of natural material to varying heights with more intense fuel loading. Smoke signaling was its own language.

Lumbering and quarrying were major industries at Waterfall Glen from the 1860s through the 1880s. On the appropriately named Sawmill Creek, the Ward family operated a sawmill. The quarries in Lemont and in Waterfall Glen were known for their high quality rock known as "Lemont Limestone" which was preferred for use as a construction material at the Chicago Water Tower and the Springfield State Capitol building.

The City of Chicago's famous Lincoln Park has also has a strong tie to Waterfall Glen. Prior to becoming a forest preserve, a small part of the property was utilized as a plant nursery. The 107-acres purchased and owned by the Lincoln Park Commission in 1907 were used to gather nutrient rich black topsoil. The soil was transported by railroad to Chicago and used as fill for creating the Lincoln Park area along Chicago's lakefront.

The Civilian Conservation Corps constructed the shelters, picnic areas and the dam or waterfall in the 1930s. Over the years the dam and waterfall area has been reconstructed several times.

The 120-acre Poverty Prairie is a worthy place to hike around in late summer just to watch butterflies flutter by. Flying squirrels have also been seen gliding overhead in the woods. Over the years several visitors have reported hearing the screech of a bobcat. When bobcats vocalize they make a terribly loud scream like banshees. There have been two people who have actually reported seeing glimpses of the rare "wood ghost". Because of all the contiguous Cook and DuPage County forest preserve properties in the DesPlaines River valley, it is certainly possible that there is a thriving population of this secretive animal.

There is one natural waterfall hidden in a remote location of this forest preserve. It is not marked on a map. Trail enthusiasts must find it on their own, using their own resources.

FOR MORE INFORMATION

Visit the Forest Preserve District of DuPage County website at www.dupageforest.com or telephone (630) 933-7200.

West DuPage Woods Forest Preserve Trail

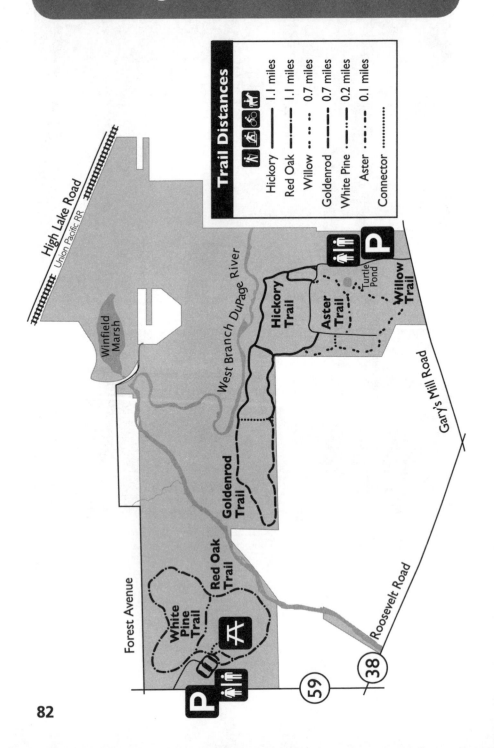

Trail Distances

	🚶 🚴 ♿ 🏇	
Hickory	——————	1.1 miles
Red Oak	–··–··–··	1.1 miles
Willow	–·· –·· –··	0.7 miles
Goldenrod	– – – –	0.7 miles
White Pine	–·· –·· –··	0.2 miles
Aster	–· –· –·	0.1 miles
Connector	··············	

High Lake Road

Union Pacific RR

Winfield Marsh

West Branch DuPage River

Turtle Pond

Hickory Trail

Aster Trail

Willow Trail

Goldenrod Trail

Red Oak Trail

White Pine Trail

Forest Avenue

Gary's Mill Road

Roosevelt Road

59

38

West DuPage Woods Forest Preserve Trail

18

WEST CHICAGO

TRAIL LENGTH

1.1 mile looped trail.

TRAIL SURFACE

Crushed limestone.

The West DuPage Woods trails are groomed for diagonal and skate style cross-country skiing when there is adequate snow cover, but is low priority on the trail-grooming list.

LOCATION

In West Chicago located on the east side of Illinois Route 59, approximately one-half mile north of Roosevelt Road.

TRAILHEAD LOCATIONS

To access the looped trail, utilize the parking area located on the east side of Illinois Route 59 in West Chicago.

The two miles of trail located on the east side of the West Branch of the DuPage River can be accessed from the north side of Gary's Mill Road between Winfield Road and Roosevelt Road.

TRAIL DESCRIPTION

The one-mile Black Oak Trail is a closed-loop trail that is joined by the much shorter White Pine Trail. There is varied terrain along the route and it is a mostly tree-lined environment that offers shade in the summer and fantastic cross-country skiing during winter because it is sheltered somewhat from the wind. The flat and sloping terrain provide opportunity for a nice lunchtime workout whether you run, hike, bike or ski. There are overlooks and good views of the West Branch of the DuPage River.

East of the DuPage River, on the north side of Gary's Mill Road is the Elsen's Hill section of West DuPage Woods. There are approximately two miles of looped trail sections comprised mostly of dirt and turf trails. The trails are steep and rugged-best suited for hiking or cross-country running or skiing.

TRAVELER'S NOTEBOOK

Accounts from the 1890s described the "wooded hillsides to the north of Gary's Mill Road as "the most popular picnic spot in the area." The West Branch of the DuPage River runs through West DuPage Woods Forest Preserve and brings the opportunity to view a great variety of wildlife species. More than 230 native plant species inhabit this biologically rich forest preserve. There are a few high-quality wetland areas called fens that grow native skunk cabbage, a plant known to begin growing through the snow cover in early February. During early spring months many species of woodland flowers including Dutchman's breeches, May apple, spring beauty and wood anemone are in abundance.

The oak, hickory and maple woods provide homes for the southern flying squirrel. The squirrel doesn't actually fly but instead it glides through the air. The squirrel measures eight to nine inches in length, and has loose folds of skin that connect forelimbs to hind legs and serves as gliding membranes. The southern flying squirrel has large black eyes and a bushy flattened tail. It is nocturnal and as a result is seldom seen by people. These nocturnal wild acrobats will glide for eighty yards or more in the hardwood canopy. It must be quite a tree top circus under the stars!

It is sunnier at the Elsen's Hill area on the east side than on the shady forested west side of West DuPage Woods. The east side also contains a small prairie remnant. During late summer, painted lady, monarch, red-spotted purple, viceroy yellow and black swallowtails butterflies are bountiful and can be watched floating and landing to feed on milkweed, asters and other forbs in flower.

Butterflies can lay up to 1,600 eggs in the course of their lifetimes. Their presence or lack thereof can be an indicator of the relative health of an ecosystem. The expansion or reduction of butterfly ranges help experts understand the effects of habitat destruction, pollution and climate change.

TRAIL TALK

The hills in the Elsen's Hill section offered winter sledding and tobogganing as early as 1866. It was a tree-lined hill cozily tucked inside a wooded area where local kids and families would gather with their sleds and flyers. It was originally named Boie's Hill perhaps named after its original owner. In the 1960s and beyond locals would called it Boy's Hill or Elsen's Hill and all ages would come day and night to slide down its slippery slopes. Upon arrival warming fires could be smelled from the small gravel parking lot.

Eventually in the 1970s a legitimate fire ring was added and fire wood was routinely delivered by rangers. Improvements were made so that toboggans would have a specialized chute with a drop gate and lights were installed along the toboggan run. The hill was kept open until ten o'clock during winter weekend nights when there was adequate snow cover.

During the 1970s as the area's population grew, the hill's popularity increased to the point where it wasn't uncommon to have more than 8,000 visitors on a single, snowy weekend. It became so overcrowded that on a day late in the season after a thaw and freeze the hill was icy and wicked fast. After the eighth ambulance victim arrived at Central DuPage Hospital's emergency room, a hospital representative called the supervising ranger and requested that he cease operating the hill. The Elsen's Hill sled and toboggan runs were closed in 1980 due to safety concerns and erosion damage. At the time of closure, divots and scars from sled collisions could be observed in many of the trees' trunks lining the sled hill.

FOR MORE INFORMATION

Visit the Forest Preserve District of DuPage County website at www.dupageforest.com or telephone (630) 933-7200.

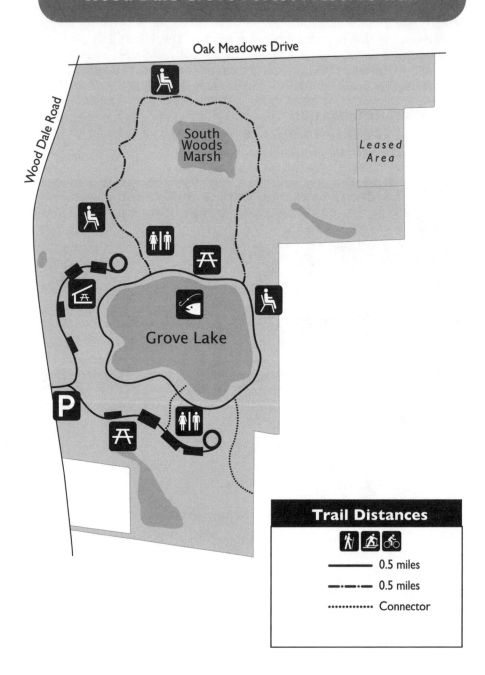

Wood Dale Grove Forest Preserve Trail

Oak Meadows Drive

Wood Dale Road

South Woods Marsh

Leased Area

Grove Lake

P

Trail Distances

——— 0.5 miles

—·—·— 0.5 miles

············· Connector

Wood Dale Grove Forest Preserve Trail

19

WOOD DALE

TRAIL LENGTH

1.1 mile

TRAIL SURFACE

Crushed limestone.

LOCATION

Wood Dale Grove in Wood Dale is located on Wood Dale Road, between Lake Street (U.S. Route 20) and Third Avenue, west of Illinois Route 83.

TRAILHEAD LOCATIONS

Hikers and bicyclists should use the parking lot on the east side of Wood Dale Road.

TRAIL DESCRIPTION

This is definitely an easily accessed 1.1-mile looped trail. The parking lot is very close to the trail and is generally used by lots of young riders, walkers, and people with strollers or wheelchairs. It incorporates a nice view of the nine-acre Grove Lake with the oak woodlands in the background.

This trail is flat as a pancake with no sharp turns. The trail system surrounds the Grove Lake and meanders through restored woodlands. The looped trail around the lake is visible from any vantage point and is great for young riders who want to wander the trail independently but can still remain under the watchful eyes of a supervising adult.

TRAVELER'S NOTEBOOK

This 179-acre grove is peaceful and scenic. It has all the amenities necessary for an afternoon of great exploring, hiking or learning how to ride a bike. The grove's facilities include fine mowed picnic areas, two reservable picnic shelters, two handicapped-accessible fishing piers, a water pump and two sets of primitive style restrooms.

The fully accessible fishing piers offer an opportunity to fish while out over the water, away from the lakeshore. Grove Lake reaches a maximum depth of twenty-eight feet and has been stocked with several species of game fish. Hundreds of rainbow trout are stocked every April and October. The fish are easy to catch on some days and they provide lots of excitement for first-time fishermen when they strike. The limit is five trout per day and if you are sixteen years of age or older you must have a fishing license and trout stamp. Fishing is always a fun diversion for children and adults who need a break from riding the looped path.

TRAIL TALK

Wood Dale Grove Forest Preserve is home to an interesting forest community called flatwoods. Flatwoods have all the habitat characteristic of a healthy forest including mature trees, shrubs and plants growing on the forest floor. According to Jack McRae, a naturalist with the Forest Preserve District of DuPage County, "flatwoods are formed on level ground, with a thick layer of impermeable clay several feet below the surface that traps rainwater. Swamp white oak and basswood grow well in poorly drained soil. The characteristic plants of the shrub understory include winterberry, dwarf raspberry, serviceberry, nannyberry and wild black currents."

Because of their flatness, the woods pool water in small temporary ponds. These isolated ponds may only last through the early weeks of spring. Before drying up they serve as a sort of singles bar for amphibious creatures. Wood frogs and blue-spotted salamanders are just a couple of the rare species that call flatwoods home.

FOR MORE INFORMATION

Visit the Forest Preserve District of DuPage County website at www.dupageforest.com or telephone (630) 933-7200.

Willowbrook Forest Preserve and Wildlife Center

20

GLEN ELLYN

TRAIL LENGTH

0.8 mile of looped trail best for strolling and hiking.

TRAIL SURFACE

0.5 mile crushed limestone, and 0.3-mile asphalt.

LOCATION

Willowbrook Forest Preserve and Wildlife Center's entrance is located on the east side of Park Boulevard at Fawell Boulevard (formerly 22nd Street) across from the College of DuPage. It is approximately one mile north of Butterfield Road and is located at 525 S. Park Boulevard in Glen Ellyn.

TRAILHEAD LOCATIONS

The main entrance at 525 South Park Boulevard is the only access point to this forest preserve. The parking lot is located on the east side of Park Boulevard.

TRAIL DESCRIPTION

Two short trails are of special interest to hikers and nature lovers. Bicycling is discouraged due to trail width and the amount of families, school and youth group trail traffic. There is a short 0.3-mile asphalt loop trail that gives people a close-up view of native northern Illinois wildlife such as bald eagles, golden eagles, red-tailed hawks, great-horned owls, red and grey foxes, raccoons and many other critters. All the animals on exhibit have injuries or conditions that prevent their release back into the wild.

A crushed limestone trail with a one-half mile interior loop has the wildlife exhibits and informative and interesting signs that explain wildlife habitats. Benches along the way offer a chance to sit back and observe nature. The butterfly garden is a spectacular highlight during the summer months. Did you know that a caterpillar's first meal is often its own egg shell? And that after emerging from its chrysalis, a butterfly needs to stand still and allow its wings to dry before it can fly?

The outermost trail is a one-half mile crushed limestone looped nature trail. Interpretive signs describe plant succession, local geology and woodland, wetland and prairie habitats. The trail is mostly flat and easy for novice and young trail trekkers to negotiate.

TRAVELER'S NOTEBOOK

Willowbrook Wildlife Center is a wildlife rehabilitation and education center. More than 4,000 injured or orphaned animals are brought to Willowbrook each year for care. Many education programs provide learning experiences for visitors to help them live in closer harmony with their wildlife neighbors.

Highly qualified and dedicated staff members and volunteers attend to the animal patients. Once an animal's health has been restored, it is released back into its native habitat, usually in a DuPage County Forest Preserve.

Domestic animals and non-native species, such as house sparrows, pigeons and starlings are not accepted for treatment. Willowbrook staff members do not make "house calls" to people who are having a wildlife crisis in their attic, chimney or under the deck! They will always take time to discuss and help deal with animal adventures on the phone or in the wildlife center.

Late spring and early summer is baby season at Willowbrook Wildlife Center. There are viewing windows inside the exhibit building. Visitors can watch volunteers and staff members specially prepare wildlife meals of seeds, crayfish, crickets, meal worms to feed raccoon and fox kits, ducklings, turtles, possums, songbirds and other species. Several indoor exhibits house area songbirds, blue jays and wetland avian species in naturalistic cage settings. It is an interesting place and you will probably spend more time watching wildlife and reading signs than hiking.

TRAIL TALK

Animals in nature are in a daily survivor episode. Occasionally we might be lucky enough to view predator prey relationships when there is a sharp-shinned or Cooper's hawk attack on the juncos or sparrows feeding at the backyard birdfeeder. Death from above happens in a flashing cloud of feathers unless an animal has a defensive strategy.

The great horned owl, a powerful predator in its own right, can be threatened by something larger than itself. The raptor ruffles its feathers spreads its wings, pitches forward with talons in an attack ready position and begins swaying back and forth. The clacking of its beak combines with the posturing to discourage any further aggression by a potential predator.

Young great horned owls occasionally get blown out of their nests during windy spring weather or fall out of a tree when at the juvenile stage and "branching out" into the tree area outside of the nest. Forest preserve arborists wearing safety helmets and other gear are called on to hoist the owlets in a bucket into the tree canopy and place them in the original nest or on a temporary wood platform nest.

Turkey vultures are well-known scavengers of road kill and are becoming a more common sight in DuPage County. The turkey vulture's defense is crude and offensive. The bird will vomit a partially digested meal of road kill to discourage a predator. The putrid smell and stench that land on a victim drive it away.

Many amphibians and insects have bad taste. For example, if a toad is captured, it will blow its body into a larger form, tuck its nose under its body exposing mostly warty skin that secretes an irritating chemical that affects the mucous membranes of most animals that might be inclined to try a toad meal. Nature is a serious survival contest, but for humans it can be entertaining to observe from a distance. as well as many golden eagle, red-tailed hawks, great-horned owl, red and grey fox, raccoons and many other critters. All the animals on exhibit have injuries or conditions which prevent them from being released back into the wild. A crushed limestone trail with a one-half mile outer loop has interpretive signs that explain wildlife habitats. Benches along the way offer a chance to sit back and observe nature. The butterfly garden is a spectacular highlight during the summer months.

The outermost trail is a one-half mile, crushed limestone, looped nature trail. Interpretive signs describe plant succession, local geology and woodland, wetland and prairie habitats. The trail is mostly flat and easy for novice and young trail trekkers to negotiate.

FOR MORE INFORMATION

Visit the Forest Preserve District of DuPage County website at dupageforest.com or telephone Wiilowbrook Wildlife Center at (630) 942-6200.

TRAIL COURTESY

Ride under control at all times and be predictable, as if a family of five is just around the next bend in the trail.

Communicate with other wayfarers by talking and using hand signals. Treat everyone with courtesy and respect.

Announce your changes in direction. If you are passing others say, "I'll be passing on your left" in a loud, low registered voice. Say a word of thanks or greeting as you pass by.

Ride in single file and stay to the right side of the trail.

Scan the ground twenty to thirty feet in front of you, and look up at what's ahead.

Keep an eye out for what is going on behind you; a rear view mirror is a great safety feature.

Keep a safe interval between you and what's up ahead.

Move off to the side of the trail after making a complete stop.

Slow down near animals of any kind.

Wheels always yield to heels and hooves (hikers and horses).

Horses cannot see directly ahead, so move to one side in order to be seen as you approach.

Try to be quiet and not interrupt those who are watching wildlife and communing with nature.

Use a light if you are riding after sunset or when it is dark. DuPage County Forest Preserve trails are open from one hour after sunrise until one hour after sunset.

Stop, stretch, wave and be friendly.

Leave the trail looking nicer than you found it. Recycle and pick up some litter.

TRAIL TRAVEL ESSENTIALS

Personal Identification	Tire Pump	Bandana
Bike Helmet	Tire Levers	Chain Oil
Money	Energy Food	Sunscreen
Cellular Phone	Wrench	Insect Repellent
Water	Patch Kit	Sunglasse
Bike Lock	Allen Wrench Set	
Spare Inner Tube(s)	Spoke Wrench	

Regional Trails

West Branch Regional Trail

21

TRAIL LENGTH

The West Branch Regional Trail will be approximately twenty-three miles completed.

TRAIL SURFACE

Crushed limestone with short sections of asphalt.

LOCATION

Upon completion the West Branch Regional Trail will run from the north end of DuPage County and connect with Will County trails at the south end. It will generally follow along the West Branch of the DuPage River.

TRAILHEAD LOCATIONS

From the southern part of DuPage County there are access points at Pioneer Park in Naperville, McDowell Grove Forest Preserve in Naperville, Warrenville Grove in Warrenville, Blackwell Forest Preserve in Warrenville, West Branch Forest Preserve in Bartlett and Mallard Lake Forest Preserve in Hanover Park. There will be several additional access points as additional segments of the trail are constructed.

TRAIL DESCRIPTION

The West Branch Regional Trail will extend through twelve DuPage County forest preserves, sixteen community parks and several important historic and cultural sites. The planned multi-purpose trails will provide links to existing and future trails that will form together to establish a network of trail systems into and through neighboring communities. As it stands now there are approximately ten miles of trails to enjoy traveling in the northern and southern parts of DuPage County. More miles of trails are added each season.

The Forest Preserve District currently has laid out more than eight miles of trail along or near the West Branch of the DuPage River in southern DuPage County. The City of Naperville bikeway will join the West Branch Regional Trail at McDowell Grove's south boundary at Ogden Avenue (U.S. Route 34). From McDowell Grove the rail will continue south of Ogden Avenue toward the Naperville Riverwalk, Pioneer Park and 1.8 miles beyond. A new 32-car parking lot offers accessibility at Pioneer Park in Naperville and to the south. Plans include extending the trail to an underpass at 75th Street and beyond.

The longest section of existing trail begins in southwestern DuPage County at the parking lot of the 426-acre McDowell Grove Forest Preserve in Naperville. This portion follows a part of the West Branch of DuPage River. During the 1930s the Civilian Conservation Corps dredged, shaped and widened areas of the river to create islands, a dam and other scenery. Three-quarters of a mile north toward Mud Lake, a stand of trees including sugar maple, red oak, hackberry, ash, basswood and paw paw challenge an amateur arborist's identification skills. Here, the trail continues north under Diehl Road and Interstate 88 before crossing Warrenville Road and entering Warrenville's historic district at Second Street.

The old Methodist Church on the west side of Second Street became the art studio used by famous artists Adam Emory Albright and his twin sons Ivan and Malvin. The former church and artist studio is now home to the Warrenville Historical Society and Museum. The Warren Tavern also on the west side of Second Street is a historic restoration in progress.

After a short jog west on Main Street, the trail enters Warrenville Grove Forest Preserve, where it curls through an open grove near the low-head dam, winds up a hill, over a bridge and merges with the Illinois Prairie Path. A right, or easterly turn, onto the Illinois Prairie Path takes adventurers to the corner of Winfield Road and Butterfield Road (Illinois Route 56), where trail users must cross Butterfield Road to gain access to Blackwell Forest Preserve and its more than seven miles of trails.

Eventually the next and trickiest piece of the regional trail, the central or middle section will be constructed. The proposed West Branch Regional Trail will continue north from its present terminus at Gary's Mill Road at Blackwell across Roosevelt Road (Illinois Route 38) through the 460-acre West DuPage Woods Forest Preserve in West Chicago, the 360-acre Winfield Mounds Forest Preserve in Winfield and the 1,110-acre Timber Ridge Forest Preserve in Winfield. Upon completion, this new eight to ten-mile section will offer an ideal venue for hiking, biking, cross-country skiing, horseback riding, wildlife watching, fishing and relaxing along the West Branch of the DuPage River. This area is both biologically and topographically diverse with scattered wetlands, hardwood forest, savanna, riverine and prairie landscapes that include rolling terrain and a couple steep hills.

In the northwestern section of DuPage County there are two West Branch Regional Trail segments that are in different stages of completion. At the 632-acre West Branch Forest Preserve on the west end of Fair Oaks Road near Lies Road, a new twenty car parking lot and trailhead begins the excursion through open grasslands and past the 40-acre Deep Quarry Lake and the eleven acre Bass Lake. This area offers visitors drinking water, restroom facilities, picnic areas, fantastic fishing opportunities and a 1.6-mile trail section joins the Bartlett Bike Path.

In order to provide for different visitor-use patterns, sections in and near the adjoining 1,165-acre Hawk Hollow Forest Preserve have been built with different trail surface types. An asphalt trail built by the village of Bartlett extends nearly two miles alongside of Bartlett and Schick roads. The forest preserve's 1.88-mile limestone section stretches out in serpentine curves near the West Branch of the DuPage River from Struckman Boulevard west to County Farm Road.

For the rugged trail trekker, there is a looped, natural turf-hiking trail to explore by foot. At this open grassland it is not uncommon to see and hear grassland bird species, such as bob-o-link, eastern meadowlark, killdeer and common nighthawk. It is also a great locale to spot raptors-like red-tailed hawks, rough-legged hawks, northern harriers and kestrelsæsoaring and kiting overhead on hunting forays along the river corridor and grass-lands.

TRAVELER'S NOTEBOOK

Both the West Branch and Hawk Hollow forest preserve segments connect with community bike paths in Hanover Park and Bartlett as well as the trails winding through Mallard Lake Forest Preserve.

Eventually, this completed trail system will connect with DuPage County's North Central Regional Trail and it will join other trails on the east side of the county.

Each season more trail sections are added to the West Branch Regional Trail system. The trail will intersect with the Illinois Prairie Path, Great Western Trail and Northern DuPage County Trail.

Winfield Mounds Forest Preserve features a wood-chipped footpath that leads through an oak and hickory forest to three Woodland Period American Indian burial mounds. Interpretive signs posted at the site explain the four archaeological excavations that took place during the last century. Timber Ridge Forest Preserve, which can be reached via a spur off the Great Western Trail, is home to Kline Creek Farm, an 1890s living history farm that features a variety of interpreted family oriented seasonal activities, picnic areas, a visitor center with modern sanitation facilities.

North Central DuPage County Regional Trail

22

TRAIL LENGTH

The North Central DuPage Regional Trail will be thirty-five miles long when completed.

TRAIL SURFACE

Asphalt and crushed limestone.

LOCATION

Northern DuPage County, both on-street and off-street.

TRAIL DESCRIPTION

The North Central DuPage Regional Trail is a thirty-five mile trail that will extend from east to west in the northern portion of DuPage County. From the east the trail connects to the Salt Creek Trail Cook County's and into Ned Brown/ Busse Woods Forest Preserve and the Schaumburg bikeway system. The on-street, off-street route travels west through the communities of Bloomingdale, Roselle, Hanover Park, Bartlett and Wayne terminating into the Illinois Prairie Path-Elgin Branch on the west. From the Illinois Prairie Path Elgin Branch, trail users will be able to access the Fox River Trail where travel can continue north or south in Kane County.

This long-term project is being coordinated and worked on with communities, park districts, the Forest Preserve District of DuPage County, the DuPage County Division of Transportation, and Illinois Department of Transportation.

Several bridges and trail connections complete miles of trails connections through the Village of Roselle and Bloomingdale and Meacham Grove Forest Preserve. The Village of Hanover Park pathway system connects at Greenbrook Boulevard to Mallard Lake Forest Preserve trails system and the forest preserve's regional trail connects into Hawk Hollow Forest Preserve west of County Farm Road.

TRAVELER'S NOTEBOOK

Although miles of this trail are located off roadways and easy for any rider or hiker to negotiate, several sections are on roads with only bike path signage marking the route. Although the trail coordinators have done their best to route the trail route down streets that have reduced traffic volumes there are no bike lanes or pavement markings on some street routes. Travelers must be conscious of traffic, be very safety-minded and follow all rules of the road when using the on-street routes. Large groups and young bike riders are advised to avoid the on street routes.

FOR MORE INFORMATION

Contact Director of Public Works, Village of Roselle at (630) 980-2020 or www.roselle.il.us

---

STREET SMARTS

Follow the rules of the road.

Ride in a predictable manner.

Ride in single file and don't block traffic.

Ride with traffic and not against it.

Follow the traffic direction on one-way streets. Twenty percent of bike-versus-car collisions occur from bicyclists going the wrong way.

Communicate with other forms of traffic by talking and using hand signals.

For a left turn, point your arm and hand to the left.

For a right turn, bend your arm at a 90-degree angle with your hand and arm pointing upward.

For a stop, bend your arm at a 90-degree angle, with your hand pointing downward.

Obey all traffic signs.

Yield to pedestrians and be friendly. Walk your bike if there are lots of people.

Always park and lock your bike at a bike rack or other appropriate locations.

Keep an eye out for what is going on behind you and look at what's ahead.

Watch out for the "door zone"æthat three or four foot area next to parked cars.

Watch out for vehicles backing out of driveways. Approximately thirty-three per cent of all bike crashes happen on sidewalks!

Yield to traffic, and remember most bike accidents (and deaths) happen at intersections.

Use bicycle safety head and rear lights if low light conditions exist, for example if it is foggy, getting dark, early morning or getting dark.

Treat everyone with courtesy and respect.

Southern DuPage County Regional Trail

23

TRAIL SURFACE

The regional trail surface is asphalt and crushed limestone.

LOCATION

Southern DuPage County on-street and off-street.

TRAIL DESCRIPTION

The Southern DuPage County Regional Trail extends west to east across the southern portion of DuPage and will create a link between Aurora and Hinsdale and Burr Ridge.

According to the DuPage County Division of Transportation the trail includes the following features:

Creates a forty-six mile regional trail linking to existing off-road trails and bikeways (on street and off-street) in several communities and the Forest Preserve District of DuPage County.

Contains a mixture of bikeway facility types including off-road paths (similar, for example, to the Illinois Prairie Path), on-street designated bicycle lanes, and on-street signed bicycle routes (provided through roadway shoulder improvements).

Includes a main stem trail running from Aurora to Woodridge branching into three spurs in Woodridge including a main stem traveling a northern route, the Greene Valley Forest Preserve Spur and the Waterfall Glen Forest Preserve Spur.

The trail connects eleven communities, Aurora; Naperville; Woodridge; Darien; Bolingbrook; Downers Grove; Westmont; Clarendon Hills; Willowbrook; Burr Ridge; Hinsdale and unincorporated areas of Naperville, Lisle, and Downers Grove Townships.

Completed links include U.S. Route 34 (Ogden Avenue) 75th Street from Frontenac to Illinois Route 59, Aurora; 75th Street from Modaff to Washington Street, Naperville; Springbrook Prairie Trail (by Forest Preserve District); trail segment along Madison Street segment south of Plainfield Road (in conjunction with the roadway improvement project) and Hobson Road. Segments along a portion of 83rd Street in Woodridge and Darien, along Plainfield and 75th Street in Downers Grove, Darien and Willowbrook along Clarendon Hills Road in Willowbrook, Darien and unincorporated Downers Grove Township, and along 101st Street with an entrance to Waterfall Glen Forest Preserve at Lemont Road.

TRAVELER'S NOTEBOOK

Although miles of this trail are located off roadways and easy for any rider or hiker to negotiate, several sections are on roads with only bike path signage marking the route. The trail coordinators have done their best to route the trail route down streets that have reduced traffic volumes. Bike lanes or pavement markings are absent on some street routes. Travelers must be conscious of traffic, be very safety minded and follow all rules of the road when using the on-street routes. Large groups and young bike riders are advised to avoid the on street routes.

FOR MORE INFORMATION

Contact DuPage County Trail System Coordinator, at (630) 407-6883 or visit www.dupageco.org

Salt Creek Greenway Regional Agencies Path

24

TRAIL LENGTH

The Salt Creek Greenway includes significant sections of open space approximately one-half mile wide on either side of Salt Creek. As part of the Salt Creek Greenway Master Plan a regional bicycle route is intended to parallel Salt Creek. It will be about thirty-five miles in length when it is finished.

Although the trail has an approved master plan it will be several years and many thousands of dollars before it is complete.

A finished northern section of the trail begins in Ned Brown Forest Preserve in northwestern Cook County and follows Salt Creek downstream to the south through the community of Elk Grove Village and then enters the northern edge of DuPage County. A proposed land trail will continue to extend south along the creek through Wood Dale, Itasca, Addison, Elmhurst, Villa Park, Oak Brook Terrace, Oak Brook and Hinsdale as well as portions of unincorporated Addison and York Township.

As the greenway crosses into western Cook County near Interstate 294, it is routed through a series of Cook County forest preserves and the communities of LaGrange Park, Westchester, North Riverside, Brookfield, Riverside and Lyons.

TRAIL SURFACE

Crushed limestone, asphalt and on-street bike routes

LOCATION

Upon completion, the Salt Creek Greenway Trail will become a regional bicycle trail extending from Ned Brown Forest Preserve in northwestern Cook County through eastern DuPage County to the Chicago Portage National Historic Site on the Centennial Trail in southern Cook County. It will generally follow a north and south direction and lie within one-half mile of Salt Creek.

TRAILHEAD LOCATIONS

Although the Salt Creek Greenway Trail has not been totally constructed and connected there are several access points near lengthy completed segments at Cook County and DuPage County forest preserves. There are also a few other locations within the boundaries of the participating municipalities that offer easy access to the completed portions of this trail.

Easily accessed locations include Wood Dale Grove Forest Preserve in Wood Dale, Cricket Creek Forest Preserve in Addison, Salt creek Forest Preserve in Addison, York Woods Forest Preserve in Elmhurst and Fullersburg Woods Forest Preserve in Oak Brook and Ned Brown Forest Preserve in Elk Grove Village (Cook County).

In the future, additional trailheads will be available for visitor use. According to the *Salt Creek Greenway Master Plan Goals and Recommendations*, "this should include the multiple use trailheads...a new bikeway trailhead at the intersection of the Salt Creek Greenway Trail and the Illinois Prairie Path, and a regional trailhead along the creek at North Avenue (Illinois Route 64)".

TRAIL DESCRIPTION

As it stands now there are approximately sixteen miles of out and back Salt Creek Greenway trails to travel in the northeastern part of DuPage County. The Wood Dale and Itasca municipal bikeway systems connect with trails to the north and extend into Cook County. This northeastern section extends through Elk Grove Village and onto trails surrounding Busse Lake at Ned Brown Forest Preserve in Cook County. The trail extends from the Oak Brook and Fullersburg Woods Forest Preserve in southeastern DuPage County into Cook County eventually terminating at 47th Street and the Des Plaines River.

Pedal-powered explorers can travel safely for approximately eight miles north from Salt Creek Forest Preserve in Addison. The route joins the Itasca and Wood Dale Bike Path and extends into Cook County, Elk Grove Village and more forest preserve green space.

The ride up and over the well-designed Irving Park Road Bridge offers a pleasant view of the Village of Itasca. The trail is in good condition and begins to enter expansive areas of reclaimed nature. The Wood Dale/Itasca Reservoir is an excellent place to conduct a speed workout. It is a circular 1.2 miles of terrifically smooth asphalt that resembles a huge bathtub. The old quarry was re-designed to accept Salt Creek's floodwaters and impound them until water levels drop in Salt Creek. This is a huge vat. Because it is so close to O'Hare International Airport the sky is full of jets or as bird watchers like to say, "greater gas hawks."

The many chords of power lines here can also affect your nature experience if you let them. The area does, however, offer some good peaks of nature especially as the path winds past Salt Creek Marsh full of herons, sunflowers, goldfinches and mallards. The trails eventually run into and join a bike route in Elk Grove Village. The on-street bike route courses through quiet residential neighborhoods and eventually arrives at Ned Brown Forest Preserve. There is an additional fifteen miles of bike trails winding around this 3,700-acre Cook County Forest Preserve. Here visitors can choose to take a break, relax, picnic, fish, watch model airplanes or the real big ones, rent a boat and paddle around on the 590-acre lake or do some more pedaling back to paradise in DuPage County.

Additional trail segments in DuPage County are located at Wood Dale Grove Forest Preserve in Wood Dale and Cricket Creek Forest Preserve in Addison. The Village of Oak Brook has developed a very safe and extensive off road path system that includes Fullersburg Woods Forest Preserve trails in Oak Brook. The Oak Brook Path is asphalt while trails through Fullersburg Woods Forest Preserve have a surface of limestone screenings. There is a combined distance of more than twenty miles of the best DuPage County trail and path experiences for family fun.

TRAVELER'S NOTEBOOK

There are already many travel destinations to pedal to along this developing greenway, bike route and trail system including; movie theaters, health clubs, nature centers, picnic areas, miniature golf courses, fishing holes, restaurants, churches, indoor and outdoor aquatic centers and of course, wildlife viewing areas.

Within the greenway are six National Registered Historic Sites. These include the **Graue Mill** (constructed in 1852), the **Graue Homestead** (built in 1880), **Benjamin Fuller House** (circa 1843), **Francis Stuyvesant Peabody Mansion** (built in 1919-21) and **Portiuncula Chapel** at Mayslake Forest Preserve, the **Villa Avenue** and the **Ardmore Avenue** Chicago, Aurora and Elgin Stations (built in the 1920s), and **Elmhurst College** (founded in 1871) to name a few.

Other intriguing historic and cultural sites include **Church on the County Line** in York Township, built in 1878; the **Ovaltine Court** building of the former Ovaltine factory in York Township constructed in 1917; **Itasca Public School House** built in 1895; **Villa Park Village Hall** and the **York Tavern**, a former grocery in Oak Brook. The York Tavern now serves a good burger and always has ice-cold beer for a bicyclist's parched throat.

TRAIL TALK

The Salt Creek Greenway will extend through nineteen Cook and DuPage County Forest Preserves, sixteen local parks and many cultural and historic sites including National Historic Register sites. The planned multi-purpose trails will provide links to existing and future trails that will form together to establish a network of trail systems into and through neighboring communities. The Salt Creek Greenway regional bicycle trail is a key link to the establishment of the 216-mile integrated trail network in Northeastern Illinois. It will also connect to the Illinois Prairie Path and the North Central DuPage County Regional Trail.

The Forest Preserve District of DuPage County is partnering together with ten public land holding agencies to develop miles of trail along or near Salt Creek. Eventually the more than thirty-five mile stretch will be constructed

The greenway provides many benefits in addition to riding and hiking including:

- Protecting and providing corridors for plants and wildlife
- Protecting cultural resources
- Increasing the value of private property for those who live nearby
- Enhancing the aesthetic appeal of neighborhoods and communities
- Buffering the Salt Creek watershed providing flood relief and improves water quality
- Portage sites improvements to provide for the development of a water trail

Hopefully, as funding is secured the additional twenty to twenty-four miles of trail will be constructed. These developments will create any key connections with the existing segments and provide longer and safer trails to pedal and hike.

FOR MORE INFORMATION

Visit the Forest Preserve District of DuPage County's Web site at www.dupageforest.com or telephone (630) 933-7200.

Contact the Village of Itasca at www.itasca.com or telephone (630) 773-0835.

Contact the City of Wood Dale at www.mywooddale.com or telephone (630) 766-4900.

Contact the Village of Oak Brook at www.oak-brook.org or telephone (630) 990-3000 or contact the Oak Brook Park District at www.obparks.org or telephone (630) 990-4233.

City and Village
Bikeways, Pathways
and Trails

Village of Bartlett Bike Path

VILLAGE OF BARLETT

PATH LENGTH

Approximately 20 miles.

PATH SURFACE

Asphalt.

LOCATION

Village of Bartlett.

PATHWAY PARKING LOCATIONS

Downtown Bartlett, Apple Orchard Park and other parks

PATH DESCRIPTION

The Bartlett Bike Path is awesome! It is one of DuPage County's best village Bike Path systems and it is mainly off-road making it excellent for a family outing. it is very extensive, beautiful and a very smooth ride for long stretches through community parks, forest preserves and the quaint but modern Village of Bartlett. The path has many mild hills and slopes over the rolling landscape near the West Branch of the DuPage River. Riders will enjoy sun and shade, opportunities to picnic, swim, rest, eat at a restaurant, stop at yard sale or shop at an antique shop. The riding opportunities will get even better with established path connectors into Pratt's Wayne Woods, Hawk Hollow forest preserves and James "Pate" Philip State Park

TRAVELER'S NOTEBOOK

As I rode out of town and through varied suburban neighborhoods I had that "geez I'm out in the country" feeling. The planners for the village have done a great job of winding the pathways around and through pleasant community and neighborhood parks, libraries, natural areas and views of the DuPage River. On any excursion it is likely that travelers may see deer, red fox, coyote, wood ducks, king fishers, great blue herons and other critters especially near the river and natural areas.

The area near Bartlett High School along Schick Road had some fun ups and downs to cruise. There is a route you can take to Mallard Lake Forest Preserve in Hanover Park. All told this is a nicely laid out trail system.

The beautiful community center with the adjacent public library offers food for the body and food for thought. The water park is a cool and refreshing oasis for trekkers who may be way ahead of the others or in pain and overheated. Besides the waterpark, there are areas for field sports, tennis and playground areas. It is nicely landscaped but there is also a wild seventy-five acre significant natural area to the north called Wayne Grove Forest Preserve. The grove's edge has interesting signs that describe the surrounding area's forest layers, seasonal wading bird residents and wetlands. It is a very shady grove with many large oak trees and rare woodland plants to enjoy. You could easily spend the whole day near the community park, library and nearby natural area.

TRAIL TALK

There are many community events that happen in Bartlett throughout the summer season. There was a weekend craft fair near the train station in downtown and free massages were offered to passers by. It was a hot humid day and the biking buddies were kind of sweaty and as a result, the massage therapists giving spirits were not tested to see if they could withstand such a gross massaging effort.

The Village of Bartlett offers a brochure that details the existing and proposed bike paths. For more information or to get a map call or contact:

Village of Bartlett	(630) 837-0800
Bike Path-Planning	(630) 540-4940
Bike Path Maintenance	(630) 837-0811
Bartlett Park District	(630) 540-4800

PATHS ARE CHEAP!

According to a *Chicago Tribune* article written by AP writer Emily Johns . . .

"A mile of bike path in the suburbs can cost from $100,000 to $500,000 but can grow to $1 million because of the high cost of land acquisition. A mile of freeway, by comparison can cost from $40 million to $75 million, according to the Metropolitan Council."

Village of Lisle Bike Paths

VILLAGE OF LISLE

PATH LENGTH

Approximately 7-10 miles.

PATH SURFACE

Asphalt.

LOCATION

Throughout the Village of Lisle and Green Trails Subdivision.

PATHWAY PARKING LOCATIONS

Village of Lisle Bike Route users can park at Community Park or on Main Street near the museum, train station or Village Hall. Parking areas for hikers and bicyclists intending to use Green Trails can be found near College Hill Park and Abbeywood Park on College Avenue. Trail users should also check the Web site at www.vil.lisle.il.us/explore_Lisle/Transport/LisleBike.cfm or contact (630) 271-4100. Click on *Lisle Bike Paths* and *Green Trails Bike Paths* to view maps of the trail system within Lisle.

Path Description

Lisle is blessed with an extensive bicycle and pedestrian system that includes some on-street as well as extensive off-road pathways throughout Community Park, into downtown Lisle and south to Green Trails Subdivision.

The route through Community Park is the best part of Lisle's system. It includes smooth straight paths, gentle slopes across a rolling terrain. Green Trails Subdivision pathways are mostly pancake flat as they wind throughout the subdivision in front of people's homes and occasionally through the common areas in the back of homes where residents are mowing lawns, tending gardens, barbecuing and actively engaged in serious relaxation. It was a good quality path but touring folks may feel like they are invading people's privacy and neighborhoods.

TRAVELER'S NOTEBOOK

With its uncongested paths and many entertaining diversions, Community Park is a great place to learn how to ride a bike. When learning to ride a bike has been mastered by young riders, there is a lot of other things to do at Community Park like taking a break and swimming at the ~~water~~, picnicking at a pavilion, fishing for lunker bluegill or bullheads, watching a baseball or soccer game or making an ice cream or popcorn purchase at the food concession.

The paths taken throughout the Green Trails Subdivision seemed private and without much traffic other than of the residents.

TRAIL TALK

Another special event is "Smile Days" held during late August in the downtown section of Lisle. Just for grins, this hometown festival has lots of crafters, food and drink, live entertainment and other fun producing events, activities and exhibits.

Depot Days held each September includes fun for the entire family.

FOR MORE INFORMATION

Maps of the Green Trails Bike Path and other Lisle bike paths can be reviewed at www.vil.lisle.il.us/explore_Lisle/Transport/LisleBike.cfm or contact (630) 271-4100. Lisle Convention & Visitors Bureau.

City of Naperville Hiking and Biking Routes

NAPERVILLE

The Naperville Riverwalk is probably the most popular outdoor amenity in the western suburbs. The Riverwalk winds along side of the West Branch of the DuPage River and has attracted millions of visitors each year since its installation in 1981. It provides fantastic opportunities for those who like to hike and shop or stroll and eat.

Bicycling on portions of the Riverwalk is prohibited because of the numbers of people strolling around. The Naperville community supports the Riverwalk and new sections continue to be funded, designed and built. Naperville Park District, Riverwalk Foundation, City of Naperville, Rotary Club of Naperville and Edward Hospital and the Forest Preserve District of DuPage County, are a few of the organizations and agencies that contribute in spirited fashion to the development and extension of this pathway system. For more information contact:

www.napervilleriverwalk.com
www.edward.org

PATH LENGTH
Various.

PATH SURFACE
Asphalt with some crushed limestone.

LOCATION
Throughout the City of Naperville is a fast developing network of on-street and off-street pathways.

PATHWAY PARKING LOCATIONS
Naperville Riverwalk has several community parking lots near Jackson Street near the West Branch of the DuPage River in bustling downtown Naperville.

Pioneer Park on the east side of Washington south of Hobson Road offers parking south of downtown Naperville.

Other parking locations for biking and hiking opportunities not so close to downtown are located at Knoch Knolls Park located on the east side of Knoch Knolls Road and DuPage River Park on the south side of Royce Road.

PATH DESCRIPTION

Although pathways and bike routes curl in and around Naperville, a scenic and smooth path parallels the DuPage River and extends from Pioneer Park south 1.8 miles to 87th Street. Heading north the lane-marked pathway unfurls north for one mile until it joins the street route on Loomis Street. The roundtrip is 5.6 miles with more pathways being laid out each season.

Pioneer Park is a historic and quiet riverside park with serene picnic areas laid out and constructed during the depression era by the Civilian Conservation Corps. There is drinking water available and the pit latrine style toilets are sure to add a primitive effect.

The sights along the way blend natural and urban landscapes together making it possible to see beaver, beaver lodges, a coyote searching for a cottontail meal as well as condominium residents relaxing on their balconies and decks, reading and sunning themselves.

Pioneer Park has remnants of a bridge and picnic shelter from the Civilian Conservation Corps work that took place during the Depression era. Especially interesting is a CCC-built limestone seating area on the west side of the path. It is rather overgrown with invasive buckthorn trees but would be an interesting area to restore and landscape.

The 3.6-mile Naperville Riverwalk has got to be the most popular outdoor amenity in the western suburbs. The Riverwalk winds along side of the West Branch of the DuPage River in downtown Naperville and has attracted millions of visitors each year since its installation in 1981. It provides fantastic opportunities for those who like to hike, stroll, shop and munch.

Bicycling on portions of the Riverwalk is prohibited because of the activities, events and numbers of people strolling around. The Naperville community supports the Riverwalk and new sections continue to be funded, designed and built. Naperville Park District, Riverwalk Foundation, City of Naperville, Rotary Club of Naperville and Edward Hospital and the Forest Preserve District of DuPage County, are a few of the organizations and agencies that contribute wholeheartedly to the development and extension of this pathway system.

For adventurous spirits with a desire to go gonzo and try some serious mountain bikin', Knoch Knolls Park is the best legal spot in DuPage County. Dirt, rocks, loose woodchips, exposed roots, hills, exposed roots blend together to put the "knock" in Knoch Knolls Park. This area offers a mountain biker challenge, danger and a fun adventure. Be sure to wear a helmet and tell someone that you are going "gonzo" at Knoch Knolls Park.

Well equipped mountain bike marauders routinely use these trails that wind up, down and all around through these woods near the DuPage River. They know every sharp turn, stump to jump and pair of trees that grow close enough together to peel a rider off a bike seat faster than one could say "cowabunga".

Park district officials realize there is much erosion occurring at this 115-acre park. Signs are posted warning bicyclists that it is illegal to ride in the seriously eroded bowl section.

Knoch Knolls Park is a beautiful natural area suffering from the fact it is also a mountain biker's haven. This is where preservationists' and recreationists' philosophies collide. With so many people disconnecting from nature and becoming couch taters, should more areas be available for mountain biking? The hilly single tracks definitely put participants of all ages in a highly active, aerobic state, immerse them in nature and enhance endorphin-producing fun. The disadvantage is that the activity is detrimental to natural areas.

Knoch Knolls Park also boasts of a fire ring, horseshoe pits, picnic area, restrooms, drinking water and a disc golf course.

The DuPage River Park offers approximately 3.1 miles of great hiking trails. The park is situated along side of the East Branch of the DuPage River that has a sharp bend, or oxbow, in an open valley with good opportunity for a sunrise or sunset view. Along the river, a stoic dead tree stands out like a lone skeleton in a field. During the summer months, tree swallows glide, swoop and dip for happy meals of flying bugs. The park's turf trail skirts over a narrow footbridge, near a peaceful picnic area and past an old farm pond that must hold a few huge largemouth bass. There are lots of people who come here to strut their mutt and some canines will undoubtedly be enjoying a leash free frolic. Be prepared to fend off a panting, river-soaked canine.

TRAVELER'S NOTEBOOK

The City of Naperville continues to be a partner assisting in the planning and development of the multi-use DuPage River Trail adding path sections to the eastern and western terminus of the Riverwalk. The trail is due to be paved for year around use by pedestrians and bicyclists. Naperville's portion of this trail will be approximately nine miles long when complete. To the north it will connect with the City of Warrenville and the Illinois Prairie Path and to the south the trail will extend into Will County and connect with the Virgil Gilman Trail.

Bicyclists and walkers benefit from several additional projects designed to offer new path networks in and around the city. Naperville officials envision making foot and bike travel a legitimate alternative to driving a car. A bridge to traverse Route 59 near 95th Street is planned. As part of the DuPage River Trail project an underpass is planned for 75th Street that will allow the trail to cross the busy street. An underpass on Washington Street is also being considered as part of the Washington and 75th Street intersection construction.

As a safety feature, the city is also considering countdown signals that allow path users to know how much time they have to cross the street before the traffic light changes. Flashing lights are also being installed to alert drivers to pedestrians. New ordinance regulations are written to encourage business owners to provide bike racks. Bike lanes are being painted on neighborhood streets to create pathways through the community and establish safe routes to schools and shopping areas. Naperville is becoming very biker and pedestrian friendly!

TRAIL TALK

Plank roads were the first toll roads in Illinois. The wooden pathway system was suggested to be the best way to get across the deep wet, mud and seepy routes through northern Illinois. The wooden plank road system had worked in Russia and had also been put to use in Canada.

According *The DuPage County Guide* by Marion Knoblauch: "Three main lines of plank roads were constructed out from Chicago. Following the course of the old stage route to Naperville, the first ten miles of the Southwestern were completed in September, 1848. Its owners made $1500 the first month from tolls. Early in 1850 the Southwestern reached Brush Hill (Hinsdale), and by the end of 1851 it extended as far as Naperville, from which point companies built extensions to Oswego and Sycamore. A few miles east of Naperville a branch left the main road for Warrenville and St. Charles."

Knoblauch continues to discuss the plank road era in *The DuPage County Guide* stating, "The construction of a plank road consisted of three-inch boards laid across stringers embedded in the ground and cost about $2,000 per mile. Toll gates were set up at intervals of five miles, at the termination points of each corporation's stretch of highway. The toll-rate allowed by law was 2.5 cents per mile for a man on horseback, double that for a single team and wagon, and 7.5 cents for a four-horse vehicle. By 1851 some of the plank roads were paying 40 percent to their investors, and the editor of the Chicago *Democrat* declared them to be "the best investment afloat." But soon the heavy planks, exposed to the weather, became warped and loosened. Wagons passing over them made a tremendous clatter that could be heard "for miles around." Enthusiasm over plank roads died down as suddenly as it had taken hold." However, the tollroad concept is still with us and is an idea that will never go away.

FOR MORE INFORMATION

www.naperville.il.us
www.napervilleriverwalk.com
www.edward.org

Village of Oak Brook Path System

OAKBROOK

PATH LENGTH

The Village system is approximately seventeen miles of trail route.

PATH SURFACE

Asphalt with some crushed limestone.

LOCATION

The Oak Brook Path is the best village path system in DuPage County. Be sure to ride or hike there and see for yourself. It offers a gamut of possibilities for adventure and fun. The path system winds through the majority of the Oak Brook community, the exception being the secure, gated communities with uniquely designed, sizable and expensive homes.

Lying abreast of Salt Creek is one of the first areas settled in DuPage County, the pathway connects to interesting historic sites including York Woods the Forest Preserve District of DuPage County's first and oldest forest preserve. The inventory of historic "must sees" includes the Mayslake Forest Preserve Peabody Mansion and Portiuncula Chapel, Graue Mill and House, Old Butler School Museum and Fullersburg Woods. Trail travelers can be entertained for hours at any of these locations and should check a calendar of events to see if there are special events or programs offered.

Other intriguing and fun places to tarry along the pathway's route include The Lodge at McDonald's Campus, the beautiful outdoor shops and boutiques, luxurious hotels, Butler National or Oak Brook Golf Course, Racquet, Family Aquatic, Bath and Tennis and Premiere Fitness clubs, polo fields, community parks, forest preserves trail systems and some immense and costly mansions!

PATHWAY PARKING LOCATIONS

The Oak Brook Park District's parking lot is near the northwest corner of Forest Gate Road and Jorie Boulevard. The parking area provides easy access to the path and offers other amenities for the starting or ending your tour of Oak Brook. Other parking facilities are located at Fullersburg Woods Forest Preserve on Spring Road in Oak Brook or Graue Mill's parking lot on York Road in Oak Brook.

PATHWAY DESCRIPTION

Of all villages pathway systems planned and designed by villages and towns in DuPage County this path should receive a "Golden Pedal and Spoke Award." The Village of Oak Brook has invested heavily to provide its residents with a professionally designed and extensive network of paths. This perfectly laid out rolling asphalt path system has several under and over passes and as a result crosses only a couple busy arterial streets and the finely landscaped paths extend to all areas of Oak Brook.

According to former Director of the Oak Brook Park District, Roy Cripe, "the highlights of this trail are that it's all off road! There is no stopping and a family can keep going for long distances knowing they are on a safe route. It also includes connections to many forest preserve and you can ride to the Brookfield Zoo from the Oak Brook Path."

TRAVELER'S NOTEBOOK

There are an innumerable amount of interesting adventures that can be spontaneously created along the Oak Brook Path. All that's needed is the time to jazz up an all day or all weekend excursions. Along the route there are views of beautiful landscapes including native plantings and very formal gardens with tightly trimmed hedgerows and topiary elements. Bronze sculptures of bronze bears, fountains and gurgling brooks line the edges of long and winding hand-laid granite and brick drives.

The chance to go bird watching at a pristine nature area and see rare autos at the same time does not come along too often. At Fullersburg Woods Nature Center's parking lot it's not beyond the realm of possibility to see vintage Jaguars, Porsches and Ferraris after you have put down the binoculars and retired from watching an indigo bunting, Cooper's hawk or Blackburnian warbler.

The Lodge at McDonald's Campus offers overnight accommodations in a woodland setting that has stocked lakes for fishing, artistic sculptures along the hiking trails in the oak woods. According to Roy Cripe, "This is an unknown jewel and the restaurant's buffet is excellent." The average tab is between $12 and $20 per person.

Besides the opportunities to watch a polo match, a ride or hike to the shopping center to purchase a special something at the many unique shops can be an addition to the day's tour. There is also a great variety of restaurants. What better place could one choose to carbo-load or ingest sugars than Wild Fire, Magiones or the Cheesecake Factory?

The Oak Brook Park District's community parks are scenic and safe with an ample number of places to picnic or relax. The forest preserve trails provide quiet areas and the wildness you might enjoy after shopping and eating activities. The Graue Mill Museum and House not only relates a lot of historical information about the area, it is one of the most picturesque locations in DuPage County. Taking in the view of the old mill dam, the mill wheel churning and imagining family life and activities of the 1800s is a very pleasant way to spend a sunny spring, summer or fall day. The Village of Oak Brook is lot like Camelot. Life is always peaceful and pleasant.

TRAIL TALK

The Potawatomie Indians had a large village near Salt Creek and present day Fullersburg Woods and Mayslake forest preserves. According to the *DuPage County Guide*, "the Indian trail between Chicago and Naperville that General Scott and a detachment followed to the Black Hawk War front in 1832. Where it passed south of the Pottawatomie village on Salt Creek, the trail began to climb the gradual slope of the Valparaiso Moraine. It was not much of a hill, but it was the first one the soldiers had seen since leaving the East, and it was all covered with hazel brush. So they named it Brush Hill-or so the story goes-and the name clung to the area for many years."

In 1835 Benjamin Fuller arrived on horseback from New York and like what he saw in the Brush Hill area. After retrieving and returning with his family from Buffalo, New York and began staking is claims and knocking out a living farming and later operating a tavern near a stagecoach highway. According to the *DuPage County Guide* this area, "... was named Fuller', or Fullersburg, Tavern."

The Village of Oak Brook is a result of Paul Butler's vision and plan of action. Mr. Paul Butler became well known for his wealth and successful business dealings in developing Butler Aviation and Butler Paper Company. His dream was geared to attract upper–middle class residents and triple "A" rated business corporations, international sporting events and a one of a kind shopping center. The planned village he developed has become one of the most desirable places to live, work and play.Fox hunting was a tradition in early Oak Brook. The historical society owns many historical pictures and stories of the early hunt, and people still in the area remember those exciting days. Today the only remnant of Oak Brook's equestrian heritage is the polo matches that take place every summer at the Polo Field (where else) north of 31st Street and west of York Road.

FOR MORE INFORMATION

For more information call (630) 990-3000 or contact www.oak-brook.org.

According to a DuPage County Historical Museum 2005 exhibit
Laundry and Bicycling

During the 1890s bicycling was a national mania because of bicycles improved design and lower price young people could go off on un-chaperoned rides. Bicycles allowed flexibility and independence that horse-drawn vehicles and trains didn't offer.

Village of Woodridge Bikeways

WOODRIDGE

PATH LENGTH

The pathway system is approximately thirty-four miles long.

PATH SURFACE

Asphalt with some crushed limestone.

LOCATION

The Village of Woodridge Bikeway is for the most part an extensive off-road asphalt pathway system curling throughout the town, connecting to the parks, forest preserves, and other community facilities. There are many access points to the paths with parking, restrooms and water. Food stops in the form of quick marts and restaurants are conveniently located along the pathway system. The extensive routes are well marked with signs and pavement lane markings. Paths connect to Greene Valley Forest Preserve's multi-purpose trail system and extend through several local parks and across Commonwealth Edison right of way.

PATHWAY PARKING LOCATIONS

The Woodridge Park District Community Center located at 2600 Center Drive is a good centralized location to park. Cypress Cove Family Aquatic Park at 8301 S. Janes is a great access point and cooling off spot on the south side of the Village. If you plan to picnic before you tour the Greene Valley Forest Preserve, the parking lot is located on the east side of Greene Road between Hobson Road and 75th Street.

PATHWAY DESCRIPTION

The Village of Woodridge and the Woodridge Park District are to be commended for partnering to have a vision, create the design and construct this network of finely laid out trails in this community. The pathways offer one of the best off-road systems in DuPage County. The pathways offer many miles of ten-foot wide, off-road, asphalt pathways for pedestrians and bicyclists. The paths offer lots of sun with enough shady spots to offer all that's needed for a hard pedaling bicyclist. They are conveniently linked to residential and commercial destinations, village facilities, surrounding communities, nearby parks, golf courses, nearby forest preserves and regional trials.

TRAVELER'S NOTEBOOK

The Woodridge Parks are clean, well maintained and beautifully land-scaped. Besides visiting perfectly cared nationally acclaimed parks there are lots of things to do in Woodridge. Fishing holes, tennis courts, baseball fields, a library, picnic groves with shelters, play areas and a water park are a few of the diversions for the hiker or biker that "bonks" or wears out enjoying these wonderful pathways.

An early Saturday morning ride or hike can include many scenic views. There are lots of people starting their day out exercising on these fantastic trails. Many walkers, joggers, bicyclists and dog walkers with their canines leashed courteously share these paths. Twenty miles of pathway riding can slip by in a snap when you pedal or hike on something so smooth and nice.

The Village of Woodridge and the Woodridge Park District have an easy to understand trail brochure that has a map and explanation of the Pilot Bike Path Safety Program. The signs posted along the pathway define the route and offer guidance to bicyclists, joggers and strollers. Additional signs warn users that driveways or vehicle traffic may be present. Another great idea about this path is that posted signs are intended for the drivers of motorized vehicles to provide notice and help them understand that they are driving on a bicycle route. Pedestrian and bicyclist crossings are also marked with signs for the benefit of motorists.

The Village Bikeway Plan calls for the addition of many more pathway miles for the purposes of recreation and as an alternative transportation mode.

TRAIL TALK

One of the earliest recollections about bicycle riding in DuPage County is in a book titled *God Bless Our House* written by an early settler of present day Woodridge by the name of William Bertram Greene. "Bicycles came to us in about 1896. Father got one each for Hibbard and Laura. I was appeased by being allowed to share Laura's for which I assumed the main-tenance. Laura was most generous with that as in everything else but it was still not the same as having my own—and besides it was a girl's bicycle. The solution was slow and arduous. Father gave me a calf for my own and provided its feed. I fed it by hand while on milk—actually by finger—two fingers in fact…"

"My calf grew rapidly—it seemed slowly—and it became a heifer which is equivalent to a person becoming a teenager. It came "with calf" and in another nine months a calf was born to it and my calf thus became a cow. Fortunately, I didn't acquire a sentimental attachment to my calf as I always did to a dog or a horse—it was always my bicycle in another form.

My calf's calf brought $3.00 and my calf-cow brought $18.00. Coincidentally, my new bicycle cost $21.00. That became a possession—a part of myself. It gave me wings—a new freedom. It made the trip to school a pleasure. It made "town" accessible. It was a pleasure just to go round and round the block. Many a time did I ride up early to service, on an empty stomach, to serve as acolyte, Then Mrs. Batten or Mrs. Riddler would ask me to breakfast and I'd sing in the choir and ride home after late service. One time Hibbard and Ralph Batten planned a bicycle trip up into Wisconsin. I was younger but still included. I am still disappointed that it rained so hard that night that we had to cancel the trip and never made it at all. But it was high adventure.

Even maintenance of the bicycle was a pleasure—the care and repair of the tires, aligning the wheels, oiling, cleaning and even painting. I reconditioned and painted Laura's bicycle for Marion's use after Laura outgrew it and I believe it gave Marion as much pleasure as a new bicycle.

The first good roads movement was organized by bicyclists and that first impetus helped the automobilers who followed. The "Century Run" became a recognized achievement for bicycle sportsmen. That involved the 100-mile trip from Chicago to Elgin to Aurora and back to Chicago. It encompassed the Chicago road, or Maple Avenue north of us where Dutor's Hill was encountered. That hill was a challenge (and a subject of much cursing) especially to the advanced bicyclists who had high gear bicycles."

FOR MORE INFORMATION

For a bikeway map and more information contact: www.vil.woodridge.il.us/community/html/content_bike.html or contact the Woodridge Park District at (630) 985-0300.

Village of Lombard Madison Meadows Park

LOMBARD PARK DISTRICT

PATH LENGTH

Madison Meadows has 1.5 miles with access points at the Illinois Prairie Path and Great Western Trail.

PATH SURFACE

Crushed limestone

PARKING LOCATIONS

Parking lots for Madison Meadows Park are located on the south side of Madison Street west of Westmore Avenue in Lombard.

PATH DESCRIPTION

This short limestone based trail is approximately five to six feet wide. It is a popular walking and jogging path but also used by many young children learning to ride bikes with their parents. The path passes by play structures, basketball and tennis courts, fishing ponds and areas for field sports and picnicking.

TRAVELER'S NOTEBOOK

Madison Meadows is Lombard's largest park there is lots of wide-open landscape with hundreds of trees planted on the perimeter of field sports areas. The park is great for little tikes who want to try out their tricycles or for kids with training wheels attached to their bikes.

The disc course at Madison Meadows is intensively used. Stopping and watching this alternative sport being played is an enjoyable diversion from trekking this short path. Like traditional golfers, who have a club for every situation, disc players have several discs to choose from depending on their proximity to the hole or raised chain link basket. The clothing worn by disc golfers are not nearly as gaudy as those seen worn by golfers at public and private golf courses.

TRAIL TALK

The Village of Lombard was given an "Award for Outstanding Trailblazing." The Community Development and Public Works departments teamed together to improve safety and add trail amenities. The project improved five major street crossings of the Illinois Prairie Path and Great Western Trail

120

by adding streetlights, bike racks, trash containers, benches, drinking fountains, planters, asphalt paving and street name signs. It also included the addition of informational kiosks at major access points that posted way finding maps and newsworthy bits of information.

During the early 1800s Lombard was known as Babcock's Grove. Today it is nicknamed the "Lilac Town" because of the collection of these species of botanicals planted in Lilacia Park. During the last week of April or first weekend in May the town of Lombard has a wonderful fragrance of lilac in the air. People come from far and wide to witness the spectacle of lilacs in bloom. The town used to go so far as to have all of the police department's squad cars painted in a lilac and white color scheme. That was taking the lilac theme to the outer limit.

Thousands of visitors come to celebrate "Lilac Time in Lombard," a two-week festival in mid-May. Be sure to visit Lilacia Park and sniff out the hundreds of lilac bushes planted and blooming in late April or earl May. The grand finale of lilac time is the Lilac Festival Parade that kicks off the summer season of special events in Lombard. There is also a concert series, Saturday evening "Cruise Nights", a multi-day Taste of Lombard celebration and Fourth of July fireworks in this town of over 40,000 folks.

FOR MORE INFORMATION

Visit the Lombard Park District website at www.lombardparks.com or telephone (630) 620-7322 or telephone the Village of Lombard at (630) 620-5700 or contact www.villageoflombard.org

---

In the autumn a new danger, prairie fires, menaced the little community (near the site of present day Lombard). The Indians were accustomed, in the fall of the year, to set fire to the prairie because the high grass impeded their view. Then, too, the fire drove the wild game into the forests where it could be easily trapped. (circa 1834)

—MARION KNOBLAUCH, *DuPage County Guide*

City of Elmhurst Park District Paths

ELMHURST

ELDRIDGE PARK I BERENS PARK I WILDER PARK

PATH LENGTH

Eldridge Park paths are approximately 0.75 miles long. Wilder Park and Berens Park have short paths.

PATH SURFACE

Asphalt.

LOCATION

Eldridge Park is on the west side of Spring Road north of Illinois Route 56 or Butterfield Road in Elmhurst.

Berens Park is located on the north side of Elmhurst, south of Lake Street (U.S. Route 20) and west of Walnut Street on Gladys Avenue.

Wilder Park is located on the west side of Cottage Hill Avenue north of the Illinois Prairie Path and St. Charles Road. It is also near the corner of Church Street and Prospect.

PARKING LOCATIONS

Eldridge Park parking areas are located on the west side of Spring Road. Berens Park parking lots are located west of Walnut Avenue on Gladys Avenue inside the park boundaries.

Wilder Park has several parking areas on Prospect and Cottage Hill avenues and Church Street.

PATH DESCRIPTION

The 0.75-mile asphalt trail that encircles Eldridge Park is marked out in quarter-mile increments for joggers and walkers that calculate as they ambulate. The park has a steep hill that is set aside from the main path. The hill has a paved path to its crest.

Berens Park does not have a path system but it has fun areas where children of all ages play.

Wilder Park is a walkable museum campus and park area.

TRAVELER'S NOTEBOOK

Elmhurst Park District may well be the best-operated and managed park district in the western suburbs. The agency has won many national awards for its professionalism in the field of parks and recreation. Eldridge Park is well cared for and it has a wide variety of recreational amenities. Play areas for roller hockey, tennis, basketball, baseball, soccer and other field sports. The park is outfitted with park benches, a water fountain and portable toilets. Natural areas with native Northern Illinois prairie plants border Salt Creek and a small pond and edge the park path.

The hill converts to a sled hill when there is adequate snow cover. The hilltop has a nice view of the surrounding Village of Oak Brook and Oak Brook Terrace skyline, especially of the large, stand-alone, skyscraping office building nicknamed the "prairie penis". Enough said!

TRAIL TALK

There are several parks in Elmhurst that are worth a visit even though the paths distances are short. The 42.8-acre Berens Park on the north side of Elmhurst is well-equipped for active fun. It has five lighted baseball diamonds and soccer fields and an eight-foot wide, 9/10th's of a mile walking/running path. A recreational center named "The Hub" features an expansive, 10,000 square foot soft-surface playground with a variety of play equipment, four batting cages for softball or baseball, an 18-hole miniature golf course, and a water play or spray ground area. The Hub also has a multi-purpose room available for party rentals and other events, restrooms and a concession where visitors may purchase food, squirt guns, t-shirts, caps and other curiosities.

THE HUB'S HOURS OF OPERATION

April 1 - May 30 - 4-8 p.m. (M-F) 10 A.M. - 8 P.M. (Sat. & Sun.)
Memorial Day - Labor Day 10 A.M. - 10 P.M.
After Labor Day - October 31st 4 P.M. - 8 P.M. (M-F) 10 A.M. - 8 P.M. (Sat. & Sun.)

The 17.3-acre Wilder Park is Elmhurst Park District's oldest park. In 1936 it was publicized by the Elmhurst Centennial Historical Committee as "a garden spot as beautiful as any in the Middle West." The park is a cultural and historical center with glass greenhouses, a growing house and conservatory where plants are raised and propagated until they are of display quality.

The park includes the nationally famous Lizzadro Museum of Lapidary Art where jade and hardstone carvings can be seen and admired. The Elmhurst and Elmhurst College Art museums include collections of various artworks including Chicago Imagist, Formalist and Expressionist art. The tot lot located in Wilder Park provides a nice respite for bored kids who need large muscle group activities after getting overwhelmed looking at cultural and historical exhibits. Wilder Park is north of the Illinois Prairie Path and within easy riding distance, less than a mile away on Elmhurst's quiet residential streets.

If you have ridden or hiked in from the Illinois Prairie Path and arrive at Spring Avenue be sure to check out Stemples Cycle Center, the concession stand, summer concerts series and the family owned restaurants in this neighborhood.. It is a busy hub for people hikers, joggers and bikers using the IPP. If your bike is in need of repair the bike shop is convenient and willing to make a quick adjustment, sell you a new bike or pump up a soft tire. According to Stemple Cycle Center's owner, Michael Hudos, "Twenty-five to thirty repairs will be done on a busy weekend. I repair so many flats that I've been accused of laying broken glass out on the path." Mr. Hudos also recommends Voos Corner as a good spot to gain energy for the return trip back by consuming an ice cream cone, smoothie or frozen treat of some sort. The Spring Avenue area is shady and if the gazebo is occupied there are lots of other places to sit and rest.

Downtown Elmhurst's City Centre is another great area to walk around or relax after a long pedaling trip on the Illinois Prairie Path. The American Movie Palace Museum and the York movie theatre, restaurants, unique shops, like the magic shop and independent bookstores thrive in this well-shaded and quaint atmosphere of fountains and comfortable seating plazas. There are also many seasonal events and festivals to take part in throughout the year. Visitors to Elmhurst may also join a walking tour of the historical homes and neighborhoods.

FOR MORE INFORMATION

Contact Elmhurst Park District at (630) 993-8900 or www.epd.org
Elmhurst Art Museum at www.elmhurstartmuseum.org
Lizzadro Museum at www.lizzadromuseum.org
Elmhurst arts and culture at www.elmhurst.org/elmhurst/museum

Carol Stream
Park District Path

CAROL STREAM

ARMSTRONG PARK

PATH LENGTH
Armstrong's trail is 1.25 miles in length.

PATH SURFACE
Asphalt.

LOCATION
Armstrong Park in Carol Stream is north of North Avenue and west of Gary Avenue on Illini Drive.

PATHWAY PARKING LOCATIONS
Good parking can be found at 391 Illini Drive in Carol Stream.

PATH DESCRIPTION
This relatively short, paved trail connects with many recreational facilities including, field sport areas, sand volleyball and basketball courts, a roller hockey rink, tot and youth play area, aquatic center, historical museum and a caboose, picnic area and shelter, pond and island nature sanctuary.

TRAVELER'S NOTEBOOK
This is a good area to take tots who are learning to ride a bike. The trail is never crowded and could easily accommodate the veering and wobbly effort of kids learning to ride. Armstrong Park is also a nice place to jog, stroll, or try out in-line skates for the first time. Early on a weekend morning is the best time.

TRAIL TALK
Sorry, this park is not named after Lance Armstrong!

FOR MORE INFORMATION
Contact Carol Stream Park District at (630) 784-6100 or www.csparks.org

City of Wheaton
Park District Paths
WHEATON

ATTEN PARK | COMMUNITY PARK | COSLEY ZOO
LINCOLN MARSH NATURAL AREA | NORTHSIDE PARK
SEVEN GABLES PARK

PATH LENGTHS
Vary

PATH SURFACE
Crushed limestone and asphalt

LOCATION
Atten Park is north of Butterfield Road (Illinois Route 56) on the northwest side of Wiesbrook Road in the northwestern part of Wheaton.

Community Park is located on the north side of Wheaton on the east end of Thornhill and north end of President streets.

Cosley Zoo is located west of Gary Avenue northwest of downtown Wheaton.

Lincoln Marsh Natural Area is on the western edge of Wheaton adjacent to the Elgin Branch of the Illinois Prairie Path.

Northside Park is located on the north side of Wheaton (duh!) at the northern end of West Street.

Seven Gables Park is located on the eastern edge of Wheaton on the west side of Naperville Road between Naperville and Roosevelt Road

PATHWAY PARKING LOCATIONS
Atten Park parking lots is located north of Wiesbrook Road and Warrenville Avenue intersection

Community Park main parking lot is located at the east end of Thornhill Street and a secondary parking area is at the north end of President Street.

Cosley Zoo parking area is on the south side of the Gary Avenue and Jewell Road intersection.

Lincoln Marsh Natural Area main parking area is located at the Pierce and Harrison avenue intersection. This natural area's trailhead parking lot is at the west end of Lincoln Avenue

Northside Park main parking area is located at the north end of West Street. There is a second parking lot at the intersection of Darling Street and Armbrust Avenue.

Seven Gables Park parking area is located on the west side of Naperville Road north of Blanchard Street. Another parking area is at Winnerscop Drive north of Brighton Drive.

PATH DESCRIPTION

Some Wheaton Park District's parks contain significant natural areas and others are intensely developed with facilities and have well-manicured landscapes. Every park has its own unique character and variety of park amenities are usually connected by short lengths of pathways.

Atten Park (39.60 acres), Community Park (68 acres) and Seven Gables Park (66.5 acres) are carefully managed, safe and accessible. The paths vary in distance as they weave and wander among the numerous recreational amenities. Each park's facilities include a drinking fountain, clean washrooms, shady and serene picnic areas, shelters, open grass fields for active games and sports play, tot lots, playgrounds, basketball and tennis courts.

Atten, Northside (69.6 acres) and Seven Gables parks have vita courses consisting of a series of exercise stations. Other parks might have special features such as, community gardens and ponds and wetlands that make for good fishing or ice skating during the winter months.

Cosley Zoo (11.8 acres) with an extensive paved pathway system is pedestrian friendly and accessible neighborhood zoo. Because of the number of visitors watching the critters it is not a good place to ride a bike. The 135-acre Lincoln Marsh Natural Area has woodchipped trails that require sturdy shoes and a hardy spirit.

TRAVELER'S NOTEBOOK

The Wheaton Park District staff, volunteers and commissioners have developed an award-winning parks system that is dedicated to providing fun for everyone. The Lincoln Marsh is wild and diverse. It has a Teams and Ropes Course that can offer hours of adventure to groups who want to bond and challenge their physical, social and psychological limits. The marsh also offers a quiet to relax and appreciate wetland wonders. Dragonflies, butterflies, muskrats, coyotes and deer can be enjoyed from seating areas and overlooks. This park is adjacent to the Elgin Branch of the Illinois Prairie Path and makes a great loafing area for those who need a break from pedaling or hiking.

Cosley Zoo is open year around and offers a chance for kids and adults to get up close and personal with wild and domestic animals. The zoo and park district staff members do a great job of placing animals in comfortable, natural settings where they can feel like they are in their home habitats but still be easily seen by visitors who come expecting to see them. Deer, fox, owls, turtles, ducks, goats, horses, llamas and cows are part of this living exhibit. The winding path is accessible for wheel chairs, strollers and large groups. Bicycling is not an option.

This small neighborhood zoo is very close to the Illinois Prairie Path but there is no direct route without going onto the busy Jewell Road or Gary Avenue.

TRAIL TALK

According to several accounts, including one in *The DuPage County Guide,* during 1857 the City of Naperville and Wheaton residents struggled with the question of which town should be the county seat. Although Naperville was the county seat many saw that Wheaton should be the seat because it was centrally located and it had a railroad. In June 1867, Warren Wheaton successfully led convinced members of the state legislature to move the county seat from Naperville to Wheaton because it was more centrally located. Residents of "Naperville refused to admit defeat and flatly declined to give up the courthouse records, in spite of injunctions, which were answered by instituting counter proceedings. Then came the fatal morning in July 1868."

"Hiram H. Cody and his family, who lived opposite the Naperville court-house, awakened to see the men's forms moving silently up and down the broad courthouse steps. Some carried lanterns; the others, armfuls of something they were putting into a wagon that stood in the road. Cody knew what that something was. Skipping out the back way, he ran over to the Congregational Church, where he rang the bell in wild alarm. The Wheaton faction stationed a guard around the home of James M. Vallette, then deputy county recorder, and seized him when he tried to get over to the courthouse…"

"Naperville's plan to recover its loss by force were circumvented by her president, Lewis Ellsworth, and County Sheriff James J. Hunt. Informed of the party being assembled at a saloon for the purpose of counter attack, the two officials devised a scheme to prevent what they considered a fool-hardy escapade. They went to the saloon and pretended to enter into the conspiracy. With false generosity, they bought drinks for each of the active participants in such rapid succession that one by one the heroes allowed them-selves to be escorted home quietly. Last to relinquish the chance of serv-ing his town on the field of honor was the man delegated to furnish transportation. Only by telling him that his team would be shot on the streets of Wheaton, could he be deterred from his noble aim."

FOR MORE INFORMATION

Contact Wheaton Park District at (630) 665-4710 or visit the website www.wheatonparkdistrict.com.

City of Westmont Park District Path

WESTMONT

TY WARNER PARK

PATH LENGTH
Approximately one mile.

PATH SURFACE
Asphalt

LOCATION
Ty Warner Park in Westmont is located east of Cass Avenue (also named Midwest Road in Oak Brook) between Ogden Avenue and 31st Street in Oak Brook. It is approximately one block east of Cass Avenue on Chestnut Street. There is a parking lot located approximately one half block away if you turn right on Burr Oak Drive.

TRAIL DESCRIPTION
Ty Warner Park has a beautiful, smoothly laid-out asphalt trail that curls around the perimeter of this thirty-six acre park. This park offers a fantastic mix of natural areas and highly landscaped and developed areas. With a sled hill, wetland, tot play and spray areas, sand volleyball court, large shelter with a flagstone fireplace, fountain, Veteran's Memorial, ball fields, prairie, gazebo and woods there is a fun spot for everyone. It is the only park I've found that has a bocce court.

Three interpretive signs are placed alongside the path at intermittent spots around the pond. One sign offers an explanation about how deep-rooted prairie plants can hold shorelines together better than shallow rooted mowed bluegrass.

Another compares oceans of water to oceans of prairie with waves, schooners and vastness. The third sign relates the value of preserving wetlands.

The path offers a great learn to ride spot for young bicyclists or tricyclists. It also offers easy accessibility for wheel chairs and strollers. The scenery is great and there is a lot of fun to be had at Ty Warner. Pack a picnic and your favorite Beanie Baby and go see this wonderful place.

TRAVELER'S NOTEBOOK

Ty Warner Park is named after the community-minded and generous collectible toy manufacturer that is headquartered within view of this open space gem. On the day I visited, a woman who was walking her dog pointed out that the executive offices overlooked the park and there was significant interest and sponsorship offered by the Warner group as the park property was purchased, designed and built. So she continued to say that it was no coincidence that the color scheme of Ty Warner Park matches the Ty Warner corporate office. The roofs on the shelter, gazebo and other structures are the same blue color that highlights the office building. Even the complimentary doggie doo-doo bags (aka, mutt mitts) available at the trailhead are that same color blue!

While I visited this fine park visitors were pouring in. Joggers, dog walkers and hikers were all attracted to this facility. Comfortable benches were occupied by couples taking in the wonderful scenery and watching all the fun stuff people were engaged in.

TRAIL TALK

Westmont received its name due to the fact it was an elevated mound located between Lake Michigan and the Mississippi River valley. After the Great Chicago Fire a person by the name of William Greggs capitalized on this location and "established the Excelsior brick making firm beside the clay pit there. The reconstruction of Chicago was facilitated by these building blocks from Gregg's Station, as Westmont was first called, they were placed on the Burlington cars and the gravity of the downhill slope d"rew the heavily laden train into the city."

The legendary great blues musician, Muddy Waters (McKinley Morganfield) made his home and raised his family in Westmont. The Westmont community has honored the blues artist by naming the four-acre Muddy Waters Park in his honor. Go there for a hike and "Get Your Mojo Working!"

FOR MORE INFORMATION

Visit the Westmont Park District website at www.wpd4fun.org or call (630) 969-8080.

Menacing and Not-So-Menacing Road Cycling Routes

Bicycle travel on DuPage County roads can be a harrowing experience. When you try to devise a list of recommended routes or a rating system you recognize in a nano-second that no road is created equal or perfectly safe. Traffic volumes will change depending on the time of day. Road shoulders are paved in some areas; road widths narrow and affect suburban bicycle travel.

All roads have different risk conditions that must be assumed and faced by the bicyclist.

Many communities print maps with recommended routes and each season it is advisable to check out different communities' websites to see what routes are now being recommended. Change is constant especially in the world of bike routes and road construction. Hopefully in the future our traffic planners will think carefully about including safe corridors for on-road bicyclists.

In any event a bicyclist must use good judgment and obey the traffic regulations on all roads. There is a lot of room for improvement for bicyclists in this regard. Motorists most frequently comment about two things bicyclers do that causes driver aggravation. First, some bicycle riders ride abreast of one another and do not ride single file. This condition impedes the flow of traffic and forces drivers to move into oncoming traffic lanes, which in turn causes a dangerous condition.

The second most-cited driver complaint is that many (not all) bicyclists do not stop at stop signs and signals. Taking into account that most bicycling accidents and most serious injuries occur at roadway intersections it is a matter of survival for bicyclists to be cautious at every intersection and understand that stop means stop. Remember that as a bicyclist you are accountable and responsible you're your own actions and safety!

Based on interviews with experienced cycling road warriors here's a take on roads that are difficult to impossible to ride. And, a list of those considered as a good escape or transportation routes based on road width, paved shoulders, lighter traffic volumes, good sight distances, minimal truck traffic, road smoothness and other favorable conditions. In all cases less experienced riders may be best advised to purchase a bike rack and drive to a trailhead.

Merciless Roads (Beyond Category Rides)

Roads traveling in a general East and West Direction

75th Street
Maple Avenue
55th Street
63rd Street
Montgomery Road
75th Street
Ogden Avenue (U.S. Route 34)
New York Avenue
North Aurora Road

Roosevelt Road (Illinois Route 38)
North Avenue (Illinois Route 64)
Butterfield Road (Illinois Route 56)
Fullerton Avenue
Geneva Road
St. Charles Road
Army Trail Road
Lake Street (U.S. Route 20)
Irving Park Road (Illinois Route 19)

Roads traveling in a general North and South Direction

York Road
Illinois Route 83
Highland Avenue
Lemont Road
Illinois Route 53
Swift Road
Glen Ellyn Road
Naperville Road
Washington Street

County Farm Road
Winfield Road
Book Road
Naperville Plainfield Road
River Road
Raymond Road
Illinois Route 59
Eola Road

Cycling Routes for Road Warriors

Roads traveling in a general East and West Direction

It is best to ride these routes early in the morning on weekends when traffic volumes are reduced.

31st Street
Bartlett Road
Diehl Road

Roads traveling in a general North and South Direction

Finley Road (north of the
   Yorktown Shopping area)
Fairview Avenue
Meyers Road
Bloomingdale Road
Lambert Road

Main Street (Wheaton)
Schmale Road
Gary Avenue
Prince Crossing Road
Mill Street

"Merciful Most of the Time" Routes

Roads traveling in a general East and West Direction

Warrenville Road

Mack Road

Batavia Road

Main Street (West Chicago)

Smith Road

"Okay Most of the Time" Routes

Roads traveling in a general North and South Direction

Park Boulevard

West Street

Leask Lane

College Road

Yackley Avenue

Herrick Road

Weisbrook Road

Indian Knoll Road

Klein Road

Modaff Road

87th Street

Munger Road

Powis Road

Exploring DuPage County

There are many educational get-aways and museums worth exploring in DuPage County. Those destinations near or along side of a trail or bike path system are marked with an asterisk. Some are easily accessed through residential areas and streets with low volume traffic but others are more difficult to get to by hiking or biking.

These historical museums, cultural and natural history centers offer fun and entertaining programs and countless unique and valuable opportunities to learn about DuPage community history, culture and nature. These places are hidden wonders along the hike or ride. Get connected to your community and offer them support.

This quick reference guide will provide a location, telephone number, or Web address (when available) for the site listed. Since fee structures and donations change frequently it's best to call ahead to find out the cost and find out whether a biking or hiking excursion is practical. A quick phone call or Web site visit can offer you up to the minute details about the next special event or new exhibits.

For up to the minute information about DuPage County's "Magnificent Miles West of Chicago" dining, shopping, calendar of events and sports contact the DuPage Convention and Visitors Bureau at (630) 575-8070, (800) 232-0502 or www.dupagecvb.com.

Arabian Knights Farm
6526 Clarendon Hills Road
Willowbrook, Illinois 60514
(630) 323-3482
Professional horse training, riding instruction, boarding, leasing and equine related special events

*Argonne National Laboratory
U.S. Department of Energy
9700S.Cass Avenue
Argonne, Illinois 60434
(630) 252-2000
www.anl.gov/welcome.html
Site of the advanced proton source X-ray project and one of the world's premier facilities for energy related research and development

* Indicates that the museum is close to a trail or bike path system.

Historical Museum Of Addison

131 W. Lake Street
Addison, Illinois 60101
(630) 628-1433
www.addisonadvantage.org/history/historicalsite.htm
Built in 1892, the Historical Museum of Addison is also known as the Balzer House and is named after one of Addison's first families.

Bloomingdale Park District Museum

108 S. Bloomingdale Road
Bloomingdale, Illinois 60108
(630) 539-3096
www.bloomingdaleparks.org/m-museum.htm
Offers seasonal exhibits of quilts, masks and other art

Carmelite Visitor Center and National Shrine of St. Therese

8501 Bailey Road
Darien, Illinois 60561
(630) 969-5336
www.sainttherese.org
This National Shrine of St. Therese, "the Little Flower," has a collection of relics and memorabilia of this venerated saint and a religious bookstore.

*Cosley Animal Farm and Museum

1356 Gary Avenue
Wheaton, IL 60187
(630) 665-5534
www.cosleyzoo.org
Cosley Zoo is a small accessible zoo that exhibits domestic farm animals and native Illinois wildlife. Visitors will find a gift shop, shaded picnic area, washrooms and seasonal concessions.

Robert Crown Center for Health Education

21 Salt Creek Lane
Hinsdale, Illinois 60521
(630) 325-1900
www.health-ed.org
Offers educational programs for all ages on human reproduction, drug abuse prevention and general health

Darien Historical Society Museum

7422 Cass Avenue
Darien, Illinois 60559
(630) 964-7033
www.darien.il.us/community/historicalsociety.htm
*Through exhibits and artifacts the Old Lace School provides detail on
Darien history. The building was also the historic home of the District #61
band department, and the Darien City Hall and jail.*

Downers Grove Historical Museum

831 Maple Avenue
Downers Grove, Illinois 60515
(630) 963-1309
*The Downers Grove Historical Society and the Downers Grove Park
District Museum are located in the same building, and share their
resources.*

DuPage Children's Museum

301 N. Washington Street
Naperville, Illinois 60540
(630) 637-8000
www.childrensmuseum.org
*Where children and adults discover, learn and play together. Enjoy
exhibits, workshops and materials that stimulate creativity and fun learning experiences.*

*DuPage County Historical Museum

102 E. Wesley Street
Wheaton, Illinois 60187
(630) 682-7343
www.dupage,co.il.us/museum
*The museum is in an 1891 Richardsonian Romanesque building, the
museum highlights DuPage County history with hands-on activities,
exhibits and an extensive model railroad display.*

*Elmhurst Historical Museum

120 E. Park Avenue
Elmhurst, Illinois 60126
(630) 833-1457
www.ehm@elmhurst.org
*This award-winning museum features changing interpretive exhibits on
Elmhurst history as well as national touring exhibits. There are programs
for children, families and adults.*

First Division Museum at Cantigny

1 S 151 Winfield Road
Wheaton, Illinois 60187
(630) 668-5161
www.rrmtf.org/firstdivision.htm
*The First Division Museum at Cantigny is dedicated to the history of the
Big Red One, the famed First Infantry Division of the United States Army.
The 38,000-square foot museum is located on the Wheaton, Illinois estate
of the late Colonel Robert R. McCormick. It includes thousands of artifacts,
life-size dioramas inside and a historical collection of tanks and artillery
pieces outside. There is also a mansion museum, beautiful gardens, a golf
course and summer musical events on the park property.*

Billy Graham Center Museum

500 E. College Avenue
Wheaton, Illinois 60187
(630) 752-5909
www.wheaton.edu/bgc/museum
*Features rare artifacts, art and displays that climax with a powerful 3-D
presentation of the Gospel message.*

William L. Gregg House Museum

115 S. Linden Avenue
Westmont, Illinois 60559
(630) 960-3392
www.wpd4fun.org/history.htm
*Victorian, red-bricked house displays collections typical of the 1920s
through 1940s in authentic lifestyle settings.*

Gretna Station and Caboose Museum

391 Illini Drive
Carol Stream, Illinois 60188
(630) 665-2311
www.carolstreamhistorical.com
*Tells the history of Carol Stream, once named Gretna, Illinois, and offers a
glimpse of railroad history.*

*Hedges Station Museum

0 N 555 Winfield Road
Winfield, Illinois 60190
(630) 510-9053
*Constructed prior to 1849 to serve Chicago to Galena Railroad this is the
oldest remaining railroad station in Illinois. It has been restored and
exhibits relate railroad and Winfield history.*

Hinsdale Historical Society Museum

15 S. Clay Street
Hinsdale, Illinois 60521
(630) 789-2600
www.hinsdalehistory.org
This restored home emphasizes the Hinsdale lifestyle prior to 1900 and exhibits depict the development of this village. The museum offers a bicycle tour of the historic village.

*Itasca Historical Depot Museum

101 N. Catalpa
Itasca, Illinois 60143
www.itasca.com/parkdistrict/programs/depotmuseum
The Itasca community's history is housed and exhibited in an 1873 rail-road depot.

*Jurica Nature Museum

Benedictine University
5700 College Road
Lisle, Illinois 60532
www.ben.edu/resources/jurica.asp
At this local field museum there are over 10,000 natural history specimens including natural habitat exhibits and an outstanding bird exhibit.

*Kruse House Museum

527 Main Street
West Chicago, Illinois 60185
www.hometown.aol.com/tlczajka/kruse.htm
The Prairie-style structure is an example of a typical middle class home of the early 1900s. Many original furnishings, quilts, clothing and jewelry are displayed.

*Lisle Depot Museum

915-925 School Street
Lisle, Illinois 60532
(630) 968-2747
The Chicago, Burlington and Quincy Railroad built this train station in 1874. Visitors enjoy the waiting room, ticket office and Lisle history while viewing historical artifacts.

*Lizzadro Museum of Lapidary Art

220 Cottage Hill, Wilder Park
Elmhurst, Illinois 60126
(630) 833-1616
www.lizzardomuseum.org
This most unusual museum has displays of Chinese jade and other hard stone carvings, dioramas, minerals, gemstones, earth science, and hands-on exhibits. Visitors can purchase geological gifts.

*Lombard Historical Museum

22 W. Maple Street
Lombard, Illinois 60148
(630) 629-1885
This Victorian home features rooms furnished with artifacts typical of the lifestyle of the emerging middle class during the 1870s.

Lynfred Winery

15 S. Roselle Road
Roselle, Illinois 60172
(630) 529-9463
www.lynfredwinery.com
For more the twenty years this quaint winery has offered wine-tastings to visitors and has sold fine wine in regional gourmet shops and restaurants. Public tours are offered on most weekends and luxurious bed & breakfast suites are available.

*Maple Street Chapel

2205 Main Street
Lombard, Illinois 60148
(630) 629-2630
www.maplestreetchapel.org
The oldest public building in Lombard features a unique American Gothic design and was built in 1870. The church belfry was used by Lombardians to view the Great Chicago Fire.

Robert R. McCormick Museum at Cantigny

1 S 151 Winfield Road
Wheaton, Illinois 60187
(630) 668-5161
www.mccormicktribune.org/cantigny/index.htm
Consisting of the Robert McCormick Mansion Museum, the First Division Military Museum, ten acres of gardens and parks, 27-hole championship golf course and nine-hole Cantigny Youth Links visitors can while away many hours at this accessible site. There are numerous musical events outdoors during summer.

*Mayslake Peabody Estate

1717 W. 31st Street
Oak Brook, Illinois
(630) 850-2363
Mayslake Peabody Estate is located within 90-acre Mayslake Forest Preserve on the south side of 31st Street in Oak Brook. Mayslake Hall was built between 1919 and 1921 for Francis Stuyvesant Peabody, a national figure in the coal industry and in Democratic politics. Mayslake Hall a 39-room Tudor-style mansion designed by Benjamin Marshall. The Portiuncula Chapel stands near the hall and is a replica of the Chapel of St. Francis of Assisi in Assisi, Italy. Each summer in the natural area, Mayslake hosts the First Folio Shakespeare Festival. Interpretive tours, plays and special event areas are offered at the site.

*American Movie Palace Museum

152 York Road
Second Floor
Elmhurst, Illinois 60126
www.historictheatres.org
The Museum contains a collection of photographs, books and memorabilia from various theatres.

*Naper Settlement Museum Village

5233 S. Webster Street
Naperville, Illinois 60540
(630) 420-6010
www.napersettlement.org
This 19th-century village with historic homes, shops, a chapel, fort and one-room schoolhouse is located in a 13-acre park-like setting with costumed villagers, exhibits and more. There are numerous special events and exhibits that occur during the year.

Sheldon Peck Homestead

355 E. Parkside Street
Lombard, Illinois 60148
(630) 6291885
This 1840s farmhouse features reproductions of Sheldon Peck's folk paintings, exhibits on the area's first school, the Underground Railroad, farming, and pioneer life.

Roselle Historic Museum

102 S. Prospect Street
Roselle, Illinois 60172
(630) 351-5300
www.roselle.il.us
The house, which hosts the museum, dates to the mid-1800s and it contains information about Roselle's history.

School & Community Assistance for Recycling & Composting Education (SCARCE)

799 Roosevelt Road
Building 3, Suite 5
Glen Ellyn, Illinois 60137
www.bookrescue.org
This environmental education center offers multitudes of opportunities to learn about conservation and the three Rs: Reduce, Reuse and Recycle. See trash turn into treasures, make recycled paper, learn what to do with those old shoes, crayons and home products. Presentations and activities are available for scouts and community groups.

Stacy's Tavern Museum

South side of Geneva Road, one-half block west of Main Street
Glen Ellyn, Illinois 60137
(630) 858-8696
www.glen-ellyn.com/historical/#stacys
This 1846 stagecoach inn and tavern presents a glimpse of life during the 1800s. Experience the art, technology and culture of northern Illinois residents.

*Villa Park Historical Museum

220 S. Villa Avenue
Villa Park, Illinois 60181
www.vphistoricalsociety.com
The history of Villa Park and the Ovaltine Company are exhibited at this Tudor-style train station. This station was originally built in 1929 by the Chicago, Aurora and Elgin interurban and sits as one of three remaining C.A. & E. stations next to the Illinois Prairie Path at its original location.

*Warrenville Historical Society Museum

3 S 530 Second Street
Warrenville, Illinois 60555
(630) 393-4215
www.warrenville.com/whis/
Once a Methodist Church, and later used as an art studio by Adam Albright and his sons, the museum offers information about Warrenville's history since 1834. It is situated along the West Branch Regional Trail.

*West Chicago City Museum

132 Main Street
West Chicago, Illinois 60185
(630) 231-3376
www.museum@westchicago.org
This museum situated in historic Turner Town Hall, is a National Register site that features local history and railroads exhibits.

*Wheaton History Center

606 N. Main Street
Wheaton, Illinois 60187
(630) 682-9472
www.wheaton.lib.il.us/whc
The museum located in a historic Queen Anne house highlights our nation's social heritage through captivating exhibits and programs. Discover Wheaton's history or experience life on the run following the Underground Railroad.

Yesterday's Farm Museum

7 N 040 Wood Dale Road
Wood Dale, Illinois 60191
(630) 595-8777
A farm complex and 1920 museum house offers visitors an opportunity to experience life in the country. Features a four-seat outhouse!

Top Ten Best Places to Hike or Bike

These rankings are based on the author's opinion and experience as a three-time dad. There is absolutely no science to the ratings and no surveys were taken to arrive at the conclusions. Consider it to be full of personal bias based on the lure of seeing domestic or wild animals, easily locating food, water, shelter, nearby shopping, flush toilets, off-road travel and other intangible or miscellaneous offerings.

★1 Waterfall Glen in Darien

Approximately ten miles of trail cut through DuPage County's most diverse landscapes. Whether it is a hike, bike or ski this is the closest you can get to a wilderness experience. Take on the bluff and enjoy a dramatic view overlooking the DesPlaines River valley, find the ancient Signal Hill and the artesian well, listen to a scarlet tanager, smell the white pine scent, get on it descending to the Sawmill Creek trail crossing and sprint across the blooming prairie full of butterflies scrolling cursive lettering in the blue sky. Go soak your head in the great outdoors, Waterfall Glen is the best!

★2 Illinois Prairie Path from downtown Wheaton to Kline Creek Farm

Eat popcorn, drink lemonade learn about DuPage County at the Historical Museum. Take trip back to DuPage County's family farm life during the 1890s. Lots of farm animals to see as you travel on flat terrain. Of course there is ice cream along the seven-mile route!

★3 Illinois Prairie Path—any Section from Elmhurst to Winfield

Depending on your endurance and energy level a trail enthusiast can travel any distance to eat, shop till you drop and visit one of several historical museums on the route. The farmers markets held in several towns make a great destination early on Saturday morning. Restroom facilities are conveniently located in restaurants and ice cream parlors along the way.

★4 Fermilab in Warrenville

Smooth asphalt trails are provided for visitors to this world famous high-energy physics laboratory located on 6,800 acres. The lab is filled with intriguing architectural, cultural, scientific and natural wonders. On the prairie there's a herd of Buffalo roaming and in winter visitors can take a gander at 15,000 Canada geese. More than 277 bird species have been spotted in the wetlands, woods and prairies. There are pieces of art inside and gigantic outdoor sculptures. The buildings feature unusual architectural designs. The electrical lines and poles resemble the Greek letter *pi*. There are more than thirty miles of roads, trails and paths at the lab.

★5 Blackwell Forest Preserve in Warrenville

Canoes, kayaks, rowboats with or without trolling motors are available for rent by the hour or half day. Climb up Mount Hoy and see hawks soar by or fly a kite. Camp, picnic, relax and watch people at DuPage County's busiest forest preserve. Search and find the flush toilets at the north parking lot or near the campground. There are many unmarked paths to discover and 6.3 miles of established trails.

★6 Morton Arboretum in Lisle

Hike and learn about botanical beauties, biking is available for members only during summer weekend evenings. Study nature, attend a special program, hear a concert, watch theatre in the woods, stop at the gift shop, eat and relax. Once you pay to become Morton Arboretum member there are 4.8 miles of trail to bicycle and more than fourteen miles of trail to hike.

★7 Willowbrook Wildlife Center in Glen Ellyn

See wildlife neighbors up close, pack a picnic and thoroughly explore the short trail. Flush toilets and changing tables are available. The indoor and outdoor wildlife museum is especially great for hikers and families with toddlers, and strollers. Leave the bicycles at homeæthere is a short exhibit trail to walk and a half-mile hiking trail.

★8 Herrick Lake and Danada Forest Preserves Trail System in Wheaton

Rent boats, fish, eat ice cream at Oberweis, see and smell wild bergamot and other blooming beauties at a restored prairie, savanna and wetland or watch horses graze at Danada Equestrian Center. Enjoy the safety of lengthy and relatively flat trails that do not cross over any roadways. The shorter distanced handicap accessible one-mile Lake Trail is a popular route for persons looking for exercise during their lunch break. The Meadowlark, Green Heron, Regional and Bluebird trails combine looped sections that expand the total distance of trails to 6.8 miles at Herrick Lake and an additional 2.8 miles of trails connecting to Danada Forest Preserve. There are flush toilets near the Danada House at Herrick Lake concession area.

★9 The Oak Brook Path System in Oak Brook

The smooth trails that seldom cross busy roads lead to the Graue Mill Museum, McDonald's Campus, Fullersburg Woods Nature Center, a scenic waterfall, picnic areas and nearby food, shopping, swimming and other scenic spaces and places. The twenty-plus miles of paths and trails add up to a fun and fantastic family outing. Flush toilets for all.

★10 Greene Valley Forest Preserve in Naperville

A few hills along the seven-mile trail add some thrills to this quiet spot. The woods are pristine and the East Brach of the DuPage River valley is pleasant and full of songbirds during spring and summer months. Wide open picnic areas with shelters offer good places for field games and the Tricky–Tree-Key program along the trails in Thunderbird Youth Campground challenge everyone's tree identification abilities.

Outstanding and Scenic Learning Places

CANTIGNY IN WINFIELD

Cantigny is the estate of Colonel Robert R. McCormick former editor and publisher of the Chicago Tribune. The former estate is now open to the public and the hours of operation vary depending on the season and the facility. There is no fee if you ride your bike or walk into Cantigny.

Cantigny is accessible from what has been termed a "carriage path" that is a limestone screening path that runs alongside of Winfield Road. The Cantigny Visitors Center, gardens and grounds, First Division Museum, golf course, youth links and tennis facility, and the Robert R. McCormick Museum can be accessed from both branches of the Illinois Prairie Path and Great Western Trail by following this sometimes rough "carriage path" that runs adjacent to Winfield Road.

Before entering Cantigny it is important to know that bicycling, roller blades and skateboards are only permitted in the parking lot areas. The distance around the perimeter of the expansive parking lots is approximately 1.1 miles. The garden paths are for walking. The Visitors Center is a good place to stop and become oriented to this unusual place. There is an orientation video to watch that explains the history of the estate and offers information about the things to do and see. Also available are restrooms, water, snacks, a gift shop and best of all, a map of the place!

The gardens and grounds are the highlight of Cantigny. You will find formal gardens and an "idea garden" where you can pick up useful tips and ideas for your own garden spot. All areas feature plant life that can grow in the midwest's climate and there is always friendly staff around to answer your questions related to growing and caring for botanical buddies. Picnic areas and nature trails are available under the canopies of tall oak trees or in the shade of manicured landscapes.

The Robert R. McCormick Museum is in Colonel McCormick's thirty-five room mansion. His grandfather Joseph Medill built a portion of it in 1896. It is open for tours by guides that provide information about the history, art, antiques and library that McCormick collected.

The First Division Museum is a museum dedicated to the men and women who have served their country. A collection of military vehicles is exhibited among the landmark oak trees in front of the museum. Tanks in the woods in Winfield look strange but definitely intrigue visitors walking the grounds on their way into the museum. Inside the museum there are dioramas and interactive exhibits that were designed to tell the story of wars from the viewpoint of those soldiers who were engaged in battle.

Cantigny Golf Course is a challenging 27-hole championship course. It also features a practice area, golf shop, clay tennis courts and fine restaurant. To attract young players to the sport a nine-hole youth course was designed and built for young duffers between eight and fifteen years of age. For more information about Cantigny visit www.cantignypark.com or call (630) 668-5161.

COSLEY ZOO IN WHEATON

Cosley Zoo is very close to the Illinois Prairie Path but there is no direct route without going onto the busy Jewell Road or Gary Avenue.

This small neighborhood zoo is open year around and offers visitors a chance to see wild and domestic animals up close and close to home. Animals are in settings where you expect to see them. The natural look inside the cages for deer, fox, owls, turtles, ducks and others make it seem less cruel that these wild things are being held in captivity. Most if not all the wildlife at Cosley Zoo are permanently injured or human imprinted and would not survive in the wild. The winding paths pass a barn with farm animals including goats, horses and llamas.

Educational programs promoting an understanding of humans and their relationship to wildlife and the environment are offered to individuals and groups. The concession stand and gift shop is worth the visit and donations ensure that this wonderful place will remain open for the future generations. Why not adopt an animal and help fund Cosley Zoo?

DANADA EQUESTRIAN CENTER IN WHEATON

Danada Equestrian Center is part of Danada Forest Preserve in Wheaton. It is located on the east side of Naperville Road approximately one mile south of Butterfield Road and three-quarters of a mile north of Interstate 88. The equestrian center is located at 3 S 503 Naperville Road in Wheaton.

The regional trail that extends east from the Illinois Prairie Path and Herrick Lake Forest Preserve travels past the center.

The equestrian center provides an opportunity for people of all ages to learn about horses. The programs are designed to teach people about the daily care and feeding of horses as well as provide them with basic riding instruction. Families and individuals needing a "stable" environment can go to the barns, visit the stable and watch horses grazing in the pastures or being trained by volunteers in the round pen.

Volunteers are a crucially important part of the center, feeding horses, mucking out stalls and cleaning tack are part of the daily chores. Danada's professional staff provides students a variety of riding programs, seminars, group tours and summer kid-friendly horse camp programs. Seasonal horse-drawn hayrides and sleigh rides are scheduled and available to all ages. Throughout the year, by advance reservation, hayrides and a bonfire are offered to private groups.

Each year on the second Sunday in October, the center opens its barn door to more than 10,000 visitors at the annual Fall Festival. Riding demonstrations, presentations of various horse breeds, food, bluegrass music, pumpkin painting and the Danada Nature Art and Photo Show are just a few of the activities hosted. Many programs and events show the importance and value of caring for our animal friends.

Most areas at the equestrian center are accessible to people who are differently-abled. Groups are welcome to use the picnic tables scattered around the facility. Modern restrooms are available near the Danada House garage. Danada Equestrian Center is open daily from 9 a.m. to 5 p.m. Call (630) 942-6200 for more information.

FULLERSBURG WOODS NATURE CENTER IN OAK BROOK

Fullersburg Woods Nature Center located on Spring Road in Oak Brook offers a variety of education programs for school-aged children, families, youth groups and adults. The primary messages revolve around connecting people to the natural resources. Many programs and events show the importance of the natural areas in DuPage County and why it is important to take care of and manage them carefully so that future generations will be able to enjoy and through a modest and wise use, preserve the beauty of nature for others.

Recently renovated, the nature center features interactive displays, including exhibits on flora and fauna of DuPage County as well as the skeletal remains of a 13,000 year-old wooly mammoth. Fullersburg Woods year-around program formats range from puppet shows, hands on nature activities, cross-country ski, hike and bike programs. Two fun and family friendly special events are the Earth Day celebration that happens around April 22nd each year and the Halloween Walk held in late October. Tickets for the Halloween Walk must be purchased early since this program is an annual sell-out.

The center is accessible to people who are differently-abled. Groups are welcome to use the picnic area and shelter. Modern restrooms are available inside the visitor center. The center is open from 9 a.m. to 5 p.m. except major holidays. Call (630) 850-8110 for more information.

GRAUE MILL AND MUSEUM IN OAK BROOK

Down the street at the intersection of York Road and Spring Road is the Graue Mill House and Museum. Long ago Frederick Graue had a house and gristmill built in 1858 and 1859. Well over a century after Graue made his family's fortune operating the mill along Salt Creek, the mill and house still stand as museum.

Visitors to Graue Mill can watch and hear Illinois' only operating gristmill crush and grind corn kernels into corn meal from April through November. Go downstairs, and one can hear and see the greased wooden gears as they groan and creak driving the millstones on the level above. Interpretative signs describe how this area was once used as an Underground Railroad for fleeing slaves traveling north. Costumed volunteers, 1860s-era furnishings and demonstrations at the mill and in the recently restored Graue house offer glimpses of what a DuPage County miller's life was like approximately 150 years ago.

The Graue Mill House is an example of Victorian Italianate architecture. The interior of the house is a multifunctional interpretive center with historical exhibits on the main level that can also be used for meeting rooms. The second level is used as office space for museum staff.

The Graue Mill has a small gift shop area that offers cornmeal, books on the history of the Fullersburg area, the underground slave railroad and related toys, postcards and other items. The Graue Mill House Museum is open mid-April thru mid-November from 10 a.m. until 4:30 p.m. Tuesday through Sunday. The mill and museum are closed on Mondays except for holidays. Call (630) 655-2090 for more information.

KLINE CREEK FARM—AN 1890s LIVING HISTORY FARM IN WINFIELD

Kline Creek Farm is an 1890s farm at Timber Ridge Forest Preserve in Winfield. The farm is located on County Farm Road, one-half mile north of Geneva Road. It is just a one-half mile hike or ride from the Illinois Prairie Path intersection of Geneva and County Farm roads and there is a ten foot wide path that leads north to the farm and connects to the Great Western Trail.

The Great Western Trail also has a path that leads south to the farm from the west side of County Farm Road. Ride south to the farm parallel with County Farm Road. The address is 1 N 600 County Farm Road in Winfield.

Kline Creek Farm is a wonderful place to see, hear, smell and touch farm life as it would have been in the 1890s. The Victorian era house, barns, smokehouse, summer kitchen, apiary, chicken coop, ice house, pump house and windmill are authentically created or accurately restored. Volunteer interpreters authentically dressed in 1890s clothes answer questions and tell stories about farm families that worked with the seasons to make a living.

The horses, Southdown sheep, chickens and shorthorn cattle are all raised and cared for by volunteers and staff members at the farm. They are considered part of this working farm and not considered as pets. Kline

Creek Farm is not a petting zoo but if you stay a while, they might ask you to do a few farm chores and sign on as a volunteer!

The programs at Kline Creek Farm follow the seasonality of making a living during the 1890s. The beauty of the farm is best experienced during Harvest Days in October. The summer's bounty from the kitchen garden, the orchard and cornfields is gathered up and made into tasty treats or feed for the livestock. In December the farmhouse is decorated for the holidays and the jolly spirit of the season can be experienced. The cozy warmth and smells emitted from the of wood burning stove, the arrangement of hand crafted gifts and authentically decorated Christmas tree are all part of the program. Occasionally the pump organ is played and everyone joins in singing or listening to the 1890s holiday music.

During March, maple sugaring takes place and visitors get to see how watery sap is gathered into buckets and then cooked down into maple syrup and maple sugar treats.

Summer events include the *Farmhands* program for children, *Evening in the Country* and glimpses into an 1890s-style Fourth of July celebration.

Most areas of the farm are accessible for people that are differently-abled. The farm is located about one-quarter mile from the parking lot. Groups are welcome to use the picnic area and shelter. There is a gift shop that offers a variety of farm merchandise. Modern restrooms are available inside the visitor center. The farm is open five days a week Thursday through Monday from 9 A.M. to 5 P.M. The surrounding Timber Ridge Forest Preserve and trail system is open every day from one hour after sunrise until one hour after sunset. The modern restrooms are available for trail users when the visitor center is closed. Call (630) 876-5900 for information.

LYMAN WOODS INTERPRETIVE CENTER IN DOWNERS GROVE

Lyman Woods Interpretive Center is a new and unique nature center in DuPage County. It is an eco-friendly designed facility that was carefully placed in a delicate 150-acre preserve of old and second growth oak woods, meadows and marsh.

The center is located west of Midwestern University and north of Good Samaritan Hospital one block east of Highland Avenue and south of 31st Street in Downers Grove. The center is located at 901 31st Street in Downers Grove. It was jointly purchased and conserved through the actions and funding of the Forest Preserve District of DuPage County, the Village of Downers Grove and the Downers Grove Park District.

In order to protect the sensitive areas and reduce the environmental impact, the interpretive center was placed in a location where several houses once stood. Design features include recycled steel supports, sealed concrete floors and lights, bathroom fixtures and HVAC on timers to create energy efficiency. The most unique feature is the prairie plant roof! The green roof reduces runoff and radiant heat, cleans water and air and acts as an insulator keeping the warm or cool air in check.

The entire preserve area is designated for nature appreciation. Although bicycling, cross-country skiing, picnicking and dogs are not allowed, the center has activities for all ages and specially requested programs can been designed with advance notice.

Lyman Woods Interpretive Center is open on a varied schedule and the grounds are open daily from sunrise to sunset. For current information call (630) 963-9388 or visit www.dgparks.org.

SPRING BROOK NATURE MUSEUM IN ITASCA

The Village of Itasca's Spring Brook Nature Center is located behind the Itasca Library and Water Park at Catalpa Avenue and Irving Park Road. The Nature Center's address is 130 Forest Avenue in Itasca. Visitors are recommended to park at the Water Park and follow the path south across the bridge to the red barn. Handicapped parking and program drop-off are available off the corner of Grove Street and Forest Avenue.

The Nature Center has more than two miles of trails for hiking through the marsh, prairie, woodland and arboretum areas. The trail advertises that visitors can walk through a tunnel of prairie grasses or stand four feet above a cattail marsh on a 700-foot long boardwalk. Along the hike there is a flowing stream, shady woods, blooming meadows and prairies, and marshes thick with cattails and swaying willows.

Spring Brook Nature Center has an aviary and Raptor Program that tells the life story and fight for survival by birds of prey such as hawks, owls, and falcons. In addition, the Raptor Program rehabilitates injured birds of prey and has an internship program.

The Center's staff and volunteers are working to recreate a native prairie on the grounds, complete with tall prairie grasses and flowering plants. The Nature Center also has a aquarium and many interactive displays and educational events about the natural world waiting to be discovered.

Call (630) 773-5572 for more information or visit Spring Brook Nature Center's Web site at www.itasca.com/index1.htm.

WILLOWBROOK WILDLIFE CENTER IN GLEN ELLYN

Willowbrook Wildlife Center is located on the east side of Park Boulevard one mile south of Roosevelt Road at 22nd Street in Glen Ellyn. It is approximately one mile south of Butterfield Road It is located at 525 South Park Boulevard in Glen Ellyn. There are no major trails close to Willowbrook Forest Preserve but it is easy to get to by riding or walking through the residential areas.

The Wildlife Center emphasizes family fun and learning about northern Illinois wildlife species. On exhibit are more than ninety injured and orphaned animals that are not suited for a life in the wild. Raccoon, fox, barred owl, great-horned owl, bald eagle, possum, turtles, frogs and snakes are just a few of the critters that hop, slither, roam around or roost inside naturalistic cage settings. Families can spend hours inside and outside looking and learning about wildlife and the humane care given to injured and orphaned wild animals.

Willowbrook offers a variety of education programs for school-aged children, families, youth groups and adults. The programs with live hawk and owls are fantastic. Wildlife Tracking, Wildlife Ecology and Sensory Awareness are also offered all year around. For the homeowner dealing with a wildlife dilemma the Willowbrook staff members can provide enough information and plans for action that will alleviate the stress that can be experienced by both humans and wildlife during a surprise or unusual wildlife encounter. Many programs and events show the importance and value of coexisting with wild animal neighbors.

The Center is accessible to people who are differently-abled. Groups are welcome to use the picnic area and shelter. Modern restrooms are available inside the visitor center. There is a small gift shop that offers nature related books and gifts. Willowbrook is open every day except major holidays from 9 A.M. to 5 P.M. Call (630) 942-6200 for more information.

Photo courtesy of Dick Todd.

Some Favorite Websites

CHICAGO ATHLETE

www.chicagoaa.com
Local news, calendar of events and opportunities for the runners, bicyclists and other outdoor-minded athletes.

CHICAGOLAND BICYCLING FEDERATION

www.biketraffic.org
The Chicagoland Bicycle Federation promotes bicycling in the region. The federation is very involved in Illinois legislative initiatives and works to make our streets safer for bicyclists by assisting in bike route design and promoting bicycling as a means of transportation.

DUPAGE COUNTY

www.dupageco.org/bikeways/bikeways&trails
(630) 407-6883
The site offers listings of special events, regional plans for trail construction, current trail construction activities, maps and DuPage County hotels and motels.

ELMHURST BICYCLE CLUB

www.elmhurstbicycling.org/
The Elmhurst Bicycle Club is active in the western suburbs of Chicago, northern Illinois and beyond. According to the group, "we ride anywhere, any time of day or night year aroundæcome join the fun!"

FOREST PRESERVE DISTRICT OF DUPAGE COUNTY

www.dupageforest.com/
(630) 933-7200
Offers complete and up to date information about forest preserves, trails, events and programs. The site offers users the opportunity to ask questions about any related topic. Responses to questions generally are received within 72 hours.

FOX VALLEY BICYCLE AND SKI CLUB

www.fvbc.org/
The Fox Valley Bicycle and Ski Club provides a focal point for the cyclist and skier for St. Charles, Geneva and Batavia and surrounding communities. The group hosts the popular Silver Springs 60 and Swedish Days rides.

GORP

www.gorpaway.com/
The site offers a backpack full of outdoor recreation information including information about hiking and camping, outdoor gear reviews, locations to hike and other informational web site links. It also provides information on rock climbing, canoeing, kayaking, mountain biking and many outdoor adventures.

LEAGUE OF ILLINOIS BICYCLISTS

www.bikeLIB.org
The League of Illinois Bicyclists is an advocacy voice for all Illinois cyclists. The group is very involved in the promotion of access, education and safety.

LEAGUE OF AMERICAN CYCLISTS

www.bikeleague.org
This group is involved in the promotion of bicycle issues on a national level. It promotes the idea of designating Bicycle Friendly Communities and promoting and coordinating Bike to Work Month.

NAPERVILLE BIKE CLUB

www.napervillebikeclub.com/
The Naperville Bike Club has an elaborate site that features ride calendars for riders of all levels, rider statistics and bicycling breaking news.

NORDIC FOX SKI CLUB

www.nordicfox.org
The Nordic Foxes promote Cross-Country skiing in Northern Illinois although most of their meetings are held in DuPage County. They plan local and out of state outings for diagonal striders and skaters for those just getting started and experts. This group has lots of fun when the snow flies.

SLACK PACKER

www.slackpacker.com
This website lists links specific to hiking websites in any state or region. Slackpacker.com also provides useful information on how to participate in geocaching and orienteering. Gear recommendations and are available.

WORKING BIKES

www.workingbikes@workingbikes.org
An all-volunteer organization, Working Bikes is a great cause, delivering bikes to people in need of a bike here and around the world—Ghana, Kenya, Nicaragua and Peru. Before wheeling an old bike out to the curb on garbage pickup day consider dropping it off at an Working Bikes drop off site. The bike doesn't have to be in working condition.

Useful Hiking Websites

AMERICAN HIKING SOCIETY

www.americanhikingsociety.org

HIKING AND WALKING HOMEPAGE

www.webwalking.com

GET OUTDOORS

www.getoutdoors.com

HIKING AND BACKPACKING

www.hikingandbackpacking.com

HIKING ILLINOIS AND INDIANA

www.hikingandbackpacking.com/illinois

ILLINOIS TRAILS AND GREENWAYS

www.americantrails.org/resources/statetrails/ILstate.html

HIKING ILLINOIS TRAILS WITH TRAIL MONKEY

www.trailmonkey.com/ilhike1.htm

Biking and Hiking Gear Web Sites

CAMPMOR

www.campmor.com

RECREATION EQUIPMENT INCORPORATED

www.rei.com

GEAR PRO

www.gearpro.com

OUTDOOR REVIEW

www.outdoorreview.com

Local Conservation and Recreation Organizations Web Sites

DUPAGE BIRDING CLUB

www.dupagebirdingclub.com

CHICAGO WILDERNESS

www.chicagowilderness.org

SIERRA CLUB, RIVER PRAIRIE GROUP

www.illinois.sierraclub.org/rpg

DUPAGE BIKEWAYS AND TRAILS

www.co.dupage.il.us/bikeways/

ILLINOIS PRAIRIE PATH

www.ipp.org

FOREST PRESERVE DISTRICT OF COOK COUNTY

www.fpdcc.com

FOREST PRESERVE DISTRICT OF DUPAGE COUNTY

www.dupageforest.com

KANE COUNTY FOREST PRESERVE DISTRICT

www.co.kane.il.us/forest

LAKE COUNTY FOREST PRESERVE DISTRICT

www.lcfpd.org

WILL COUNTY FOREST PRESERVE DISTRICT

www.fpdwc.org

ILLINOIS DEPARTMENT OF NATURAL RESOURCES

www.dnr.state.il.us

Bicycle Businesses in DuPage County

American Bicycle & Fitness
639 Ogden Avenue
Downers Grove, Illinois
(630) 971-8877

Bicycles Etc.
6460 College Road
Lisle, Illinois
(630) 369-2453
www.BicylesEtc.IL.com

Bike Line of Naperville
1277 S. Naper Boulevard
Naperville, Illinois
(630) 778-0480

*The Bike Shop
449 N. Main Street
Glen Ellyn, Illinois
(630) 793-3040
(near the Illinois Prairie Path)

Blazing Saddles Bicycles
6300 Robert Kingery Highway
Willowbrook, Illinois
(630) 986-2453

Glen Ellyn Schwinn Cycling & Fitness
460 Roosevelt Road
Glen Ellyn, Illinois
(630) 858-6400

Hartley's Cycle Shoppe Ltd.
24 W. Hinsdale Avenue
Hinsdale, Illinois
(630) 323-7156

The Hill BMX
52 W. Medinah Circle
Glendale Heights, Illinois
(630) 221-1137

*J&R Cycle & Ski
716 S. Main Street
Lombard, Illinois
(630) 620-1606
(near the Illinois Prairie Path)

Koslow Cycle Inc.
21W415 North Avenue
Lombard, Illinois
(630) 629-4773

*Midwest Cyclery
117 E. Front Street
Wheaton, Illinois
(630) 668-2424
www.midwestcylery.com
Bike rentals are available
(near the Illinois Prairie Path)

*Prairie Path Cycles
27 W 181Geneva Road
Prairie Trail Center
Winfield, Illinois
(630) 690-9749
(near the Illinois Prairie Path)

Spokes
Hawthorne Square Shopping Center
1807 Washington
Naperville, Illinois
(630) 961-8222
www.spokesbikes.com

*indicates bike business is near a trail

*Spokes
223 Rice Square at Danada
Wheaton, Illinois
(630) 690-2050
Fax (630) 690-1065
www.spokesbikes.com
(near the Danada Forest Preserve
Regional Trail)

*Stemples Cycle Center
494 Spring Road
Elmhurst, Illinois
(630) 834-1012
(near the Illinois Prairie Path)

Two Seasons Cycle & Ski
1818 Irving Park Road
Bartlett, Illinois
(847) 882-4977

Hikers and Bikers Companion

January   *Cold Month*
Be sure to start the New Year with an outdoor excursion. Even if there is a slight wind chill factor it is a good idea to start the year off with an adventure of some sort. The average temperature during January in DuPage County is 21 degrees Fahrenheit. Be sure to bundle up and dress in layers. It is surprising how warm you can stay when hiking or cross-country skiing.

On clear sunny days in January skies can produce sundogs. Sundogs are lines of rainbows on each side of the sun. Native Americans told stories about how sundogs kept the sun from going out by guarding and protecting the sun from the coldness. The straight patches of rainbows are caused by sunlight reflecting off of airborne ice crystals. When the temperature drops suddenly, the moisture in the air will condense and form a white frosting on plants and trees called hoarfrost. On cold sunny mornings it is a magnificent sight.

February   *Bony or Hungry Month*
Groundhog Day is February 2 and a tough day for most groundhogs (also known as woodchucks) to celebrate. Unless the weather has been warm they prefer to stay in their den's sleeping chamber until March. When it's hibernating a dosing woodchuck will breathe once every six minutes, and the critter's temperature may drop to 38 degrees. As it sleeps the animal uses its fat reserves and may lose up to half of its body weight during the course of a winter.

February is probably the month when the most amounts of snow falls and sticks to the ground making it the best time of year for cross-country skiing, snowman (or woman) building, sledding, tobogganing and snow angel-making. Later in the month, skunk cabbage will poke through snow in moist, wet, high alkaline areas called fens. Skunk cabbage is one of the first signs of spring!

March   *Windy Month*
How about having a contest to guess when the ice will disappear from your favorite lake or pond. Sometimes the ice will break off into elongated prisms and clink together making a chiming sound as it melts away for the season. March 20 marks the arrival of spring. With the days getting longer

and the possibility of some warmth, the great outdoors and nature liven up. No matter what the weather the first day of spring is, this is a good day to celebrate by getting outdoors for the first ride of the season or by taking a long hike.

This time of year the chorus frogs could be calling and sounding like a thumb being dragged down the teeth of a comb. Male red-winged black-birds should be perched on top of cattails laying claim to some territory with high pitched "conk-la-ree" calls and by showing off their red shoulder epaulets. Continuous flocks of sandhill cranes fly overhead looking like small letter "t's" high up in the sky circling and chortling. Flocks of ducks and geese are heading north taking rest in local ponds, lake and rivers. Take a challenge and learn to identify an American coot, wood duck, red-breasted merganser, green-winged teal and mallard.

April   *Flower Month*
By now Canada Geese have staked out their nest sites and are incubating clutches of eggs. Canada Geese defend their nest sites with a ferocious intensity. Look for the eastern bluebirds' arrival near the oak groves and fields at Fermi lab and Blackwell. Native redbud trees show the first blooms of spring. They can be spotted easily by their small reddish purple flowers growing in parks, forest preserves and yards. Many of the prairies may have received treatments of prescribed burns that promote diverse growth and to restrain fast growing invasive plants not native to these natural areas.

Celebrate Earth Day on April 22 and Arbor Day the last Friday in April by planting a redbud tree. As the redbud tree flowers fade, delicate heart-shaped leaves unfurl.

May   *Planting Month*
The woods and fields are a symphony as many varieties of warblers move, rest and migrate north through DuPage County. Male woodpeckers use their beaks to pound out long drumming solos that establish territory in their neck of the woods. Female woodpeckers drum their own sound patterns (love beats?) to communicate with these males. Woodpeckers have favorite drumming posts for their soundings. Around homes some wood-peckers may be attracted to gutters or siding that can produce loud resonating sounds. Sometimes it will occur very early on a Saturday or Sunday morning which can cause problems for people are trying to sleep.

June   *Green Corn Month*
June 21st is the first day of summer. Hikers and bikers have the longest days of the year to enjoy wayfaring. The deep "jug-o-rum" call of a bull-

frog can be heard near ponds, lakes, creeks and marshes. The sky is full of air traffic near the heron rookeries at Danada and Pratt's Wayne Woods Forest Preserves where great blue herons and great white egrets fly out and back with fish, frogs and crayfish to feed their hatchlings. Sunset hikes in late June will not disappoint as fireflies float and signal for mates above the tall grasses in fields.

July   *Corn in Tassel*

The hot humid days of July can be intense on the prairie, but a visit to West Chicago Prairie in West Chicago, Danada Prairie at Danada Forest Preserve in Wheaton, Poverty Prairie at Waterfall Glen Forest Preserve in Darien or Schulenberg Prairie at the Morton Arboretum in Lisle can be glorious. Purple cone flowers, compass plants, and black-eye Susans cover the prairie with splotches of intense color. Tiger swallow tails, monarchs and three-spotted purples drift from plant to plant or spiral up over the prairie blooms.

Coyote pups and fox kits are learning to hunt and catch prey in preparation for their litter's break up in late summer or fall. In the marshes many species of dragonflies hover and shift looking for a mate or some insect to eat. Butterfly and dragonfly field guides are available at book stores and learning about these insects can be an enjoyable diversion during your hike or bike.

August   *End of Fruit Month*

Leaves blowing in the trees sound crispy. Cottonwood trees are turning to a soft yellow or brown. Occasional leaves are falling or blowing down the paths. Many birds like the American robin, red-winged blackbirds and barn swallows are flocking. The prairies continue to erupt with colorful patterns. Crickets are chirping by rubbing their leg over coarse leg spurs and locusts are buzzing as they beat their thymbals on their sides. Orb weaver spiders spin webs each evening to snare insects that fly a fatal final route. At dawn the sun filters through the dew drops hanging on the webs.

September   *Nut Month*

In the early morning sunlight blankets of warping layers of fog shift as if the earth is breathing cool wisps of autumn air. September 23 is the first day of fall. Many bird species migrating south will fly through DuPage County this month. Acquiring a pair of binoculars and a North America bird field guide is a good idea. It is challenging to identify birds in the fall since their color is drab and less vibrant than when they migrate during spring. Pine, yellow, Nashville and chestnut-sided warblers are small, fast and challenging fun to identify. As the leaves change color look for gathering groups of nighthawks, chimney swifts, egrets and herons heading south.

October   *Harvest Month*

Play "I Caught 'em in Autumn" by bringing along a butterfly net and catching falling leaves. Inspect the leaves and see if there are galls or many color variations on each different types of leaf. Can you tell what tree the leaf fell from? Overhead there are also Canada geese honking as they fly south. If park ponds and lakes don't freeze, many of the local Canada geese remain in the area, loaf in the water and stay to nibble suburban lawns and golf courses.

Warbler traffic slows down during October, sandhill cranes, northern pintails, ring-necked ducks, buffleheads and hooded mergansers are winging through northern Illinois conservation areas. Sandhill cranes may rest overnight in fields while many species of ducks will use forest preserve marshes and waters for a rest stop. Juncos may arrive for winter feeding at neighborhood bird feeders.

November   *Big Trading Month*

With most of the leaves off of the trees a warm day in November can offer great opportunities for wildlife viewing. White-tailed deer are going through mating season and the males are in the rut, which means they are pumped up and poised for their reproductive instinct. It is an awesome sight to watch from a distance as a big buck stride with austere elegance through a woodlot to a field searching for a doe. Fox and coyote become more visible with the reduced cover in the woods.

Early in the morning or in the afternoon's fading light, the great-horned owl may fly across a field to sit in a burr oak tree and watch for prey like an eastern cottontail rabbit. Their "whoo-whoo" call and large size with horny looking tufts on their head makes them easy to identify. It is a rare sight to see a long-eared owl that winters in this area. Somewhat smaller than the great-horned owl the long-eared owl hunt in open fields and grasslands.

December   *Snow Month*

Watch the ice form over lakes, ponds and streams. The feathery patterns of clear gray ice provide a great palate for nature's artistry. A full moon with snow cover can create bright enough surroundings that an evening hike is possible without the aid of a flashlight. The first official day of winter is December 21 and the daylight period will soon be getting longer.

Rough legged hawks arrive to winter in DuPage County. The blue jay, northern cardinal, American kestrel, black-capped chickadee and downy woodpecker are a few of the year around residents living in parks, suburbs and wooded areas. With seed, berries or suet many of them can be attracted to a bird feeder. The exception, an American Kestrel, also known as the sparrow hawk, is actually a falcon and it consumes mostly mice and voles.

Trails End

In return for the good times that trails provide it is hoped that support for these quiet natural areas without stoplights, advertising and traffic noise never wanes. Trails are important assets for our community's well-being and our own lifestyles. As hikers, wayfarers, adventurers and trail bosses we must all be advocates and use our voices for logical trail connections, safe passages and the preservation and expansion of natural areas for friends and families wanting to explore. It is important to walk the walk and talk the talk.

People can and should take action on important trail issues by providing financial support or by volunteering sweat equity and helping out at workdays cleaning up, pruning and planting. We can build partnerships and energize people through attendance at workshops, conferences or by talking to friends, neighbors, community leaders and other trail trekkers. Hopefully this book has offered a good look at the accomplishments of individual and group energy applied to the specific purpose of trails. The results of positive partnerships and dedicated individual efforts have created more than 250 miles of trails and preserved more than 24,000 acres of open space for our families, friends and the next generations of trail travelers.

Bibliography

Anderson, Scott and Dierekins, Tony. *The Mosquito Book*. Duluth: Dennoch Press, 1988.

Armes, Audrie. *Here Comes The Sun*. Itasca, Illinois: Family Safety & Health, 2004.

Benyus, Janine M. *The Field Guide to Wildlife Habitats of the Eastern United States*. New York: Simon & Schuster Inc., 1989.

Bicycle Federation of Wisconsin. *Making Wisconsin a Better Place*. Madison, Wisconsin, n.d.

Bohner, Jayne. "Get It In Gear." *The DuPage Conservationist*, Fall 2000.

Bohner, Jayne. "The Trails Less Traveled." *The DuPage Conservationist*, Summer 2001.

Bohner, Jayne. "The House By the Mill." *The DuPage Conservationist*, Spring 2002.

Bystryck, Barbara. "Prairie Path Turns 40." *Daily Herald*, September 27, 2003.

Voice of the People, "Try Taking a Hike or Taking a Bike." *Chicago Tribune*, August 1, 1994.

Chicago Regional Biodiversity Council. "Biodiversity Recovery Plan," *Chicago Wilderness*, 1999.

Chicagoland Bicycle Federation. *Bike to Work Day, Week, Month & Alternative Transport Promoting And Encouragement*. Chicago 2002.

Cruickshank, Allan D. and Cruickshank, Helen D. *1001 Questions Answered About Birds*. New York: Grosset & Dunlap Publishers, 1958.

Daccordi, Mauro, Triberti, and Paolo. Zanetti, Adriano. *Guide to Butterflies and Moths*. New York: Simon & Schuster Inc., 1987.

Downers Grove Park District. *Lyman Woods*. Downers Grove, Illinois.

Dunham, Montrew and Wandschneider, Pauline. *Downers Grove 1832-1932*.

DuPage County Regional Planning Commission, in cooperation with the DuPage Mayors and Managers Conference, *DuPage County Regional Bikeway Plan Map*, 2002.

DuPage County Department of Economic Development & Transportation and Tllin International Bascor. *Proposed Improvement Plan For the Existing DuPage County Trail SystemæIllinois Prairie Path and Great Western Trail*, 2003.

DuPage County Historical Museum. *Laundry and Bicycling* exhibit, 2005.

DuPage County Division of Transportation. *The DuPage County Trail Guide, The Illinois Prairie Path, The Great Western Trail*.

Elliot, Doug. *Woods Lore And Wildwoods Wisdom*. Union Mills, North Carolina: Possum Productions, 1986.

Forest Preserve District of DuPage County. *Trails Guide*, Wheaton, Illinois 2004.

Forest Preserve District of DuPage County. *Blackwell, Churchill, Danada, Fullersburg Woods, Herrick Lake, Kline Creek Farm, Mallard Lake, Mayslake, Meacham Grove, Pratt's Wayne Woods, Tri-County State Park, Visitors Guide, Waterfall Glen, Willowbrook* brochure series. Wheaton, Illinois 2004.

Forest Preserve District of DuPage County. *Prescription Fire*, Wheaton, Illinois, 2004.

Forest Preserve District of DuPage County. *Woodlands of DuPage County* poster, 1998.

Forest Preserve District of DuPage County. "The Year of Nature in DuPage." *The DuPage Conservationist,* Winter 2002.

Forest Preserve District of DuPage County. "Trek On A Trail Today." *The DuPage Conservationist,* Spring 1996.

Forest Preserve District of DuPage County. *Fiscal Year Annual Report 2001-2002, 2002-2003,2003-2004.*

Forest Preserve District of DuPage County. *Board of Commission Meeting Minutes 2003 and 2004.*

Goben, Victoria. *Doing DuPageæA Resource Guide To County Area Museums.* September 1991.

Herrick, Frank Earl. *Poems of DuPage County.* DuPage County Historical Museum. Wheaton Daily Journal. Wheaton, Illinois, 1936.

Hesik, Kathleen. "Preserving Biodiversity in DuPage County." *The DuPage Conservationist,* Fall 2002.

Hesik, Kathleen and Weidner, Bill. "On the Right Track." *The DuPage Conservationist,* Winter 2002.

Iowa Natural Heritage Foundation. *Iowa By Trail.* Des Moines, Iowa.

Hatch, Luther A. *The Indian Chief Shabbona.* Published by Mrs. L. A. Hatch. DeKalb, Illinois, 1915.

Hochesang, Jim. *Hiking and Biking in DuPage County.* Lake Forest, Illinois: Roots & Wings, 1995.

Illinois Compiled Statutes Conservation. Illinois Natural Areas Preservation Act (525 ILCS 30).

Joyce, Denise, Chavez, Donna, Lundy, Betty and Piccinnini, Ann. "150 Fascinating Facts About DuPage." *Chicago Tribune,* March 19, 1989.

Knoblauch, Marion. *DuPage County Guide.* Wheaton, Illinois: DuPage Title Company, 1951.

Kobal, Scott. "Spring Wildflowers Nature's Gems Treasured Through The Years." *The DuPage Conservationist,* Spring 2001.

Lampa, Wayne. "West Chicago Prairie: Its Natural History and Significance." *The DuPage Conservationist,* Spring 2000.

Ludwig, Daniel. "A Place to Live." *The DuPage Conservationist,* Spring 2000.

MacRae, Jack. "In Terms Of Trees." *The DuPage Conservationist,* Winter 2003.

McCarthy, Ann E. *Critters of Illinois.* Cambridge, Minnesota: Adventure Publications, Inc., 2001.

McGrath, William Chad. *Stride and Glide.* Schofield, Wisconsin: Clear View Books, 1994.

Editors of Klutz Press. *Everybody's Everywhere Backyard Bird Book.* Palo Alto, California: Klutz Press, n.d.

Milne, Lotus and Milne, Margery. *National Audubon Society Field Guide to North American Insects and Spiders.* New York: Chanticleer Press, Inc., 1980.

Northeastern Illinois Planning Commission and Openlands Project. *Northeastern Illinois Regional Greenways and Trails Implementation Program, A Map of Greenway and Trail Opportunities and Summary.* DeKalb, Illinois, 1987.

Northeastern Illinois Planning Commission and Openlands Project. *Northeastern Illinois Regional Greenways and Trails,* Chicago 1997.

Northeastern Illinois Planning Commission and Openlands Project Paddling Council. *Northeastern Illinois Regional Water Trails Map & Plan Summary.* July 2000.

Northeastern Illinois Planning Commission and DuPage Department of Environmental Concern and Openlands Project. *Salt Creek Greenway Masterplan.* August 2001.

Puhala, Bob. *Illinois Off the Beaten Path.* Guilford Connecticut: Globe Pequot Press, 2003.

Quaife, Milo, M. *Chicago's Highways Old and New.* Chicago: D.F. Keller & Company, 1923.

Rudak, Marissa. "Keeping Warm Along The Trail." *The DuPage Conservationist,* Fall 2002.

Schirott, Beth. "Color Is In The Eye Of The Beholder." *The DuPage Conservationist,* Fall 2001.

Sullivan, Jerry. "Chicago Wilderness, An Atlas of Biodiversity." *Chicago Wilderness,* n.d.

[Staff] "Judge Frank E Herrick Dies. Noted Poet, Magistrate, Historian Succumbs at Convalescent Home." *The Daily Journal,* January 26, 1967.

"Wheaton's Beloved Poet Laureate and Police Magistrate Frank Earl Herrick Metes Out Justice and Composes Poems." *The Fox Valley Free Press,* March-April 1953.

*Thompson, Richard A., et al., *DuPage Roots.* DuPage County Historical Society, 1985.

Volker, Todd. *The Complete Grand Illinois Trail Guidebook.* Peoria, Illinois: FirstServePress, 2004.

Weidner, Bill. "When Nature Is Calling Yoo-Hoo." *The DuPage Conservationist,* Winter 2001.

Weidner, Bill. "Going With The Flow, The Making Of The West Branch Regional Trail." *The DuPage Conservationist,* Summer 2004.

Wisconsin Off-Road Bicycling Association, *Want More Trails? Join The Ride.* Elm Grove, Wisconsin.

[Staff] "Armstrong Sets Tour De France Record." Yahoo News, July 26, 2004.